Drawing Nearer to God

Women's Bible Study

by Cynthia Lanius

"Draw near to God and He will draw near to you."

—James 4:8a

ONESTONE
BIBLICAL RESOURCES

Published by:
One Stone Press
979 Lovers Lane
Bowling Green, KY 42103

Printed in the United States of America

ISBN 13: 978-1-941422-33-5

ONE STONE
BIBLICAL RESOURCES

www.onestone.com

Table of Contents

Introduction

Lesson Directions

Prior to each class do all the readings and answer the questions for that lesson *except* the application sheet. The application should be completed *after* the material in the lesson is studied in class.

Why Draw Near to God?

God makes a promise to us in James 4:8. He says if we will draw near to Him, that He will draw near to us. What an amazing promise. God isn't talking about physical proximity of course, but a life of personal, intimate fellowship with Him. Yet, this promise is conditional. It requires something on our part—we must first draw near to Him. God seeks this relationship, even to the sacrificing of His son. Romans 5:8 says, "but God shows his love for us in that while we were still sinners, Christ died for us." So the question is, do we desire this close relationship, this nearness? This study is designed to help us fulfill our part. Perhaps we should ask, "What are some of the blessings that are received from a close relationship with God?"

Being with God will bring out the best in us. Sometimes we are with people that just bring out the best in us. When we are with them, our hearts respond to their characteristics of godliness, and we behave more like them. That is how being near to God will affect us. His traits of holiness and goodness will affect us for good. We will become more like Him. He will bring out the best in us. "Oh, come let us sing to the Lord! Let us shout joyfully to the rock of our salvation. Let us come before his presence with thanksgiving: Let us shout joyfully to him with psalms. For the Lord is the great God, and the great King above all gods" (Psalm 95:1-3).

His attributes make Him wonderful to be near. Sometimes we don't want to be near someone because of the way they act, or the way they treat us. Maybe they act in a sinful manner, and it repulses us, or maybe they are mean to us. But God's nature draws us to Him. "Give thanks to the LORD, for he is good, for his steadfast love endures forever" (Psalm 136:1). Being near to God enables us to learn true goodness. He will surround us with His love and mercy. He is wonderful to be near. David said, "One thing I ask from the Lord, this only do I seek: that I may dwell in the house of the Lord all the days of my life, to gaze on the beauty of the Lord and to seek him in his temple" (Psalm 27:4).

His status makes it a great honor and privilege. "Therefore you are great, O LORD God. For there is none like you, and there is no God besides you, according to all that we have heard with our ears" (2 Samuel 7:22). If the president of the United States asked you over for a talk, imagine the honor you'd feel to be in his presence. The president wants to talk to *me*. Well, think of the majesty of the sovereign ruler of the whole world wanting you near Him. What a great honor that is. We should reflect from time to time that it is His nature—not ours—His goodness and mercy that wants us near Him. Think of the poorest, dirtiest beggar on the streets being invited to the White House; this would be amazing. Yet, it does not reach the enormous invitation that we receive when God invites us to be near Him. It is a great honor and privilege that God would want us. Jesus says, "Come to Me, all you who labor and are heavy laden, and I will give you rest. Take My yoke upon you and learn from Me, for I am gentle and lowly in heart, and you will find rest for your souls. For My yoke is easy and My burden is light."

We will learn how to be like Him. Imagine our lives without God's word. Just imagine how life might be if He had not revealed Himself to us through His word. We would look at the universe and know there must be someone who created all this (Psalm 19:1), but we would have no idea what that Creator was like. And what a mess the world would be. It is not within us to guide our own steps (Jeremiah 10:23). Can you imagine the chaos that would exist without God's direction? It is such a blessing to us that He reveals Himself to us, allows us to know Him, and allows us to learn what He wants from us and for us. Consider the words of the song "Nearer Still Nearer" on the following page.

I'm sure there are many other reasons to draw near to God, and hopefully we will pursue them in this study. We will work each day to draw closer and closer to Him.

Nearer, Still Nearer

Lyrics by Leila N. Morris, pub. 1898

Nearer, still nearer, close to Thy heart,
Draw me, my Savior—so precious Thou art!
Fold me, oh, fold me close to Thy breast;
Shelter me safe in that "haven of rest;"
Shelter me safe in that "haven of rest."

Nearer, still nearer, nothing I bring,
Naught as an offering to Jesus, my King;
Only my sinful, now contrite heart,
Grant me the cleansing Thy blood doth impart;
Grant me the cleansing Thy blood doth impart.

Nearer, still nearer, Lord, to be Thine!
Sin, with its follies, I gladly resign,
All of its pleasures, pomp and its pride,
Give me but Jesus, my Lord crucified;
Give me but Jesus, my Lord crucified.

Nearer, still nearer, while life shall last,
Till safe in glory my anchor is cast;
Through endless ages ever to be
Nearer, my Savior, still nearer to Thee;
Nearer, my Savior, still nearer to Thee!

(James 4:8; Hebrews 10:22; Psalm 73:28)

Why Daily Application?

With every lesson there are applications to be implemented. They are designed to put into practice daily what we are discussing in class. In Bible class, one of our brothers said, "Every day without God is a bad day." We want to make every day a good day, one in which we worship God and seek to please Him more and more.

It may be that you are very conscientious about preparing for your Bible class by sitting down and "getting your lesson." This is a good thing, but this class is going to be somewhat different. It asks you to think about God and think about your relationship to Him *every day*. The goal is to take what we discuss in class and apply it to our daily lives. The hope is that it will help us to draw closer to Him as we make Him a larger part of our everyday lives.

As this class begins, it is helpful to think of it as a new beginning in our lives. The human heart responds positively to new beginnings. "Therefore if anyone is in Christ, he is a new creature; the old things passed away; behold, new things have come" (2 Corinthians 5:17). When I taught high school, every student appeared excited for the new school year. I would tell them, "This is a new beginning, and all the mistakes you made last year are behind you." It is the rare student whose heart doesn't lift at the thought of a fresh start. So let's think of this class as a new start—a time to reflect on our need for God and start anew in our dedication to Him.

It's why we make New Year's resolutions—this desire for new beginnings. People often scoff at setting them because we seldom keep them, but we rarely change our behavior the first time we resolve to do so. Changing behavior most often happens in small steps rather than in giant leaps. Thoughts become acts; acts become habits; habits become character. And even then, two steps forward, one step back. And it's abundantly clear that we won't change if we don't try. We mustn't avoid making resolutions for the fear of failure. We begin this class with a new resolve to draw closer to God daily.

To do this, our goals will be two-fold. To keep them uppermost in our minds and hearts, our class goals for the series are listed on each lesson.

Class goals

- Increase our daily worship of God in praise and prayer
- Grow in grace and knowledge of God

If we use this time reflecting daily on God and on our relationship with Him, it can be the beginning of a deeper and closer walk with God that can last a lifetime. And is there any of us who do not want that?

"The tragedy of life is not that it ends so soon, but that we wait so long to begin it." (W. M. Lewis)

Why Family/Friend Discussion?

In each lesson, I ask you to discuss things with your family or friends. Why is that? I hope you can use the lessons to open a spiritual conversation with your family and friends. Seeking God is sometimes a solitary activity—your heart quietly and sincerely reaching out to God. The summary in my Bible describes Psalm 63 as "the thirsting soul satisfied in God."

> A Psalm of David, when he was in the wilderness of Judah.
> O God, You are my God; I shall seek You earnestly;
> My soul thirsts for You, my flesh yearns for You,
> In a dry and weary land where there is no water.
> Thus I have seen You in the sanctuary,
> To see Your power and Your glory.
> Because Your lovingkindness is better than life,
> My lips will praise You.
> So I will bless You as long as I live;
> I will lift up my hands in Your name.
> My soul is satisfied as with marrow and fatness,
> And my mouth offers praises with joyful lips.
> When I remember You on my bed,
> I meditate on You in the night watches,
> For You have been my help,
> And in the shadow of Your wings I sing for joy.
> My soul clings to You;
> Your right hand upholds me.

Notice the solitude described here, and yet, to fully integrate the seeking of God into our lives, we must share Him with others with whom we spend our time. If God is important to us, we will talk of Him to those we love. For some reason, this is often difficult, even for Christians. We may talk about the Bible, the church, or other spiritual things, but do we talk about God? Read Deuteronomy 6:20-25. It is all about God. It says, when your son asks you why we do these things, tell him about God. Tell him how God led us out, that He brought us into the land, that He wants to preserve us, and that we should fear Him "for our good always." Tell them about God! We need to tell others about God, and hopefully these lessons will help us open that conversation. "Can I read today's Bible reading to you?" could be a great way to start. Wouldn't it be wonderful if you could help your whole family and your friends to draw closer to God with you?

Prayer Notes

Prayer is an important part of being close to God. Because of God's rule of silence for women in the church, we are not accustomed to offering public prayer. We may pray often privately, but praying aloud among women may be intimidating. If you are using this material in a ladies' study, use the model to write a prayer, giving it meditative thought. Then the prayers can be read in class or expressed better due to the preparation having been made. It also makes an excellent model for our private prayers to help us focus more on God rather than praying selfishly.

This model contains four components:

Adoration or worship
Confession
Thanksgiving
Supplication or requests

The acronym **ACTS** helps us to remember the four parts.

Adoration is to adore God, to worship Him and to fulfill the commandment to love Him with all of our heart, mind and soul. As we spend time in adoration, we praise God for who He is. It is wonderful to begin our prayers to God with praise of Him.

I praise you for your _____

Confession/contrition allows us to clear away sins from our relationship with God. It helps us to reflect on the state of our hearts. What are our struggles, our weaknesses? What are our hurdles to putting God first in our lives?

I am sorry that I _____

Thanksgiving: Each moment God blesses us. We should thank God for His goodness and His gifts. Think especially of the wonderful spiritual gifts that we receive through Jesus Christ.

I thank you for_____

Supplication/requests: Ask God for our needs and the needs of others. Think of spiritual needs, not just physical.

I ask you for _____

Let us work to make our prayers more heartfelt, more directed to God, more centered on God, less on our physical lives and more on our spiritual lives, pouring out our hearts to Him with respect and love.

Draw Near to God

Draw Near to God: Reading

Just think of it, we are going to learn about God, to think about Him, to talk of Him, to praise Him, to meditate on His character, and to reflect on what he wants for us and from us with the goal of drawing near to Him. Knowing God can be our strongest motivation to serve Him and to submit to Him. We are focusing on the person that God is, in order to increase our desire to please Him. Maybe we don't emphasize God enough in our teaching and preaching. My husband constantly says, "It's all about God." We will talk a lot in this study about King David because He is an example to us of someone who was near to God. "I love You, O LORD, my strength. The LORD is my rock and my fortress and my deliverer, my God, my rock, in whom I take refuge; my shield and the horn of my salvation, my stronghold. I call upon the LORD, who is worthy to be praised, and I am saved from my enemies" (Psalms 18:1-3). I want to be close to God the way that David was. Don't you?

We read about drawing near to God in James 4:8, "Draw near to God and He will draw near to you." This is a promise from God, but it is a conditional promise. God wants us near Him, but He will not draw near to us until we draw near to *Him*. How do we do this? Clearly, we have to go to God's word and let Him tell us.

If we aren't near to God, then we are far away. How do we measure this distance, and what makes us far from God? "Behold, the Lord's hand is not shortened, that it cannot save, or his ear dull, that it cannot hear; but your iniquities have made a

I love You, O LORD, my strength. The LORD is my **rock** and my **fortress** and my **deliverer**, my God, my rock, in whom I take **refuge**; my **shield** and the horn of my **salvation**, my **stronghold**. I call upon the LORD, who is worthy to be praised, and I am saved from my enemies.

- Psalms 18:1-3

separation between you and your God, and your sins have hidden his face from you so that he does not hear" (Isaiah 59:1-2). So it is sin that separates us from God. We can't be near to God if we are devoted to sin. It isn't that God couldn't save them or that his hand was too short, or that He had lost his hearing. But they were the problem. Their sin was the problem.

Also, Jesus told some Pharisees and teachers of the law, "You hypocrites! Isaiah was right when he prophesied about you: 'These people honor me with their lips, but their hearts are far from me'" (Matthew 15:7-8). Our heart can separate us from God. Perhaps we are just negligent, too busy with other things to think much about God.

God wants us near Him, so much so that He gave His only Son for our salvation. Remember the dirty beggar being invited to the White House from our introduction? We are the beggar, invited into God's kingdom. He washes us by the blood of Jesus, and adopts us as His children. We are going to focus on our God who has such great love for us that He would do this for us.

Draw Near to God: Class Preparation and Discussion

Class goals

- Increase our daily worship of God in praise and prayer
- Grow in grace and knowledge of God

Things to do

1. Find a passage that gives an attribute or description of God. Read it every day. Share it with your family or friends. Bring it to class. We will create a class list to keep and use in our worship of God.

   _____

   _____

   _____

2. Read James 4:8. What is the promise from God? _____

   _____

   What is the condition to receive the promise? _____

   _____

3. Read Psalms 73:27-28. Questions for thought: How much do you long to be close to God? How much do you trust Him and declare Him?

   a. What will happen to those who are away from God? _____

      _____

   b. What does this passage say is good? _____

   c. Where was the Psalmist's trust? _____

   d. What would he declare? _____

   e. Write a psalm. God is my _____ .

      I will draw near to Him because _____

      _____

4. Read Ephesians 3:14-21.

   a. In Paul's prayer for the Ephesians, for what does he ask? (vs. 14-19)

      _____

    b.   What does Paul say God is able to do? How does He do it? (vs. 20)

    _____

    c.   What is due God? (vs.21) _____

5.   Study the reading in this lesson.

6.   Grow in grace and knowledge of God. "But grow in the grace and knowledge of our Lord and Savior Jesus Christ. To him be the glory both now and to the day of eternity. Amen" (2 Peter 3:18, ESV).

God is due all glory (Ephesians 3:21). We will focus on drawing closer to God by giving Him glory, the glory that He is due. Use the Daily Application Sheet on the next page.

Remember, study each day.

Draw Near to God: Daily Application

God is due all glory, but what does it mean to give glory to God? We should desire to be close to God not merely for what we want from it but for what we can offer to God. Is this a Bible subject that we have neglected? We will do a daily study of what it means to give glory to God. Look up "glory" and "glorify" in a concordance, or search in an online Bible. Each day, read the following verses and contemplate the glory of God. Pray each day that you will live in a way to give God the glory He is due. You may be amazed at how many times the word glory appears in God's word. Read your Bible and pray every day, and grow, grow, grow.

1. Sunday: Glory is sometimes defined as "magnificence or great beauty." In the case of God, it describes the beauty of His being, of His character. Write a verse that lists a characteristic of God that makes Him beautiful. Thank Him for this all the day long. _____

    _____

    _____

2. Monday: Glorify is sometimes defined as "to reveal or make clearer the glory of (God) by one's actions." Find a passage that tells us how we may glorify God in this way. Do something today to glorify God.

    _____

    _____

    _____

3. Tuesday: "Give God the glory" has the same meaning as to glorify Him. When we give Him glory, we are recognizing His glory or helping others to recognize it. Read Romans 4:20. Who gave glory to God in this verse? How? Are you giving God glory?_____

    _____

4. Wednesday: Read Matthew 6:13. What does this verse say belongs to God? (The English Standard Version omits this.) _____

    _____

5. Thursday: Read Psalm 19:1. What does this verse say shows the glory of God? Thank God that we might see His glory in this way._____

    _____

6. Friday: Read Isaiah 6:3. "The whole earth is full of _____ ."

7. Saturday: Write the name of a hymn that talks about the glory of God. Praise God by singing or reading the words. _____

    _____

8. Sunday: Read 1 Chronicles 16:24-28.

9. Monday: Read 1 Chronicles 16:8-11. Meditate on the words. Read these beautiful thoughts over and over.

10. Tuesday: Read Ephesians 3:21. What should God receive through the church? _____

11. Wednesday: Read Ephesians 5:25-27. How must the church be in order for it to be the glorious church (some translations say "in splendor") that Jesus will present? _____

12. Thursday: Isaiah 43:7 says that God created us for His glory. Man "glorifies" God when God's glory can be seen in our words, in our love and good works.

13. Friday: Read Romans 15:5-6. How are we to glorify God from this reading?_____

    _____

14. Saturday: These and many other passages show us that we have a responsibility to glorify God. Continue searching for passages that refer to His glory. Sometimes you will just come upon it as you are studying other topics. God blesses you in your study. Let us use our study of His beauty and glory to draw closer and closer to Him. And remember His promise that if we do, He will draw closer to us.

Believe That He Is

Believe That He Is: Reading

"...for he who comes to God must *believe that He is* and that He is a rewarder of those who seek Him" (Hebrews 11:6b).

According to this passage, two things are required to come to God. This lesson will focus on the first of those requirements—believing that He is.

Our faith is the underpinning of all our service to God. We may tend to minimize our need for strengthening our faith and move on to things that we think are greater challenges, but it is our faith and trust in God that causes us to obey Him. By faith, Abraham, Moses, Daniel, and all the other great faithful of old, obeyed in very difficult circumstances. How do we build our faith?

One way is by observing His creation. The complexity of the universe demands a designer who created the "heavens and the earth." Imagine a box of Legos being tossed out at random on a table. Then imagine them coming together by themselves to form the picture on the box. That is about as credible as the universe being formed without a designer and creator.

"You alone are the Lord; You have made heaven, the heaven of heavens, with all their host, the earth and everything on it" (Nehemiah 9:6). "He alone is God. There is none like Him among the gods. All nations should worship Him, because he made them" (Psalm 86:8-10). "The Lord is the great God and King above all gods. He made the sea and His hands formed the dry land. Worship the Lord our Maker, for He is God" (Psalm 95:1-7).

> You alone are the Lord; You have **made heaven**, the heaven of heavens, with all their **host**, the **earth** and **everything on it**.
>
> - Nehemiah 9:6

The Lord is the great God and King above all gods. He **made the sea** and His hands **formed the dry land**. Worship the Lord **our Maker**, for He is God.

- Psalm 95:1-7

A second way to build belief is by examining His word. It is faultless even though it was written by over 40 different authors from all walks of life: shepherds, farmers, tent-makers, physicians, fishermen, priests, philosophers and kings over a period of some 1,500 years, from around 1450 B.C. (the time of Moses) to about 100 A.D. (following the death and resurrection of Jesus Christ). Has any book held the importance throughout history that this book has?

A third way to build faith in God is to examine the prophecies that were fulfilled by Jesus hundreds of years after they were uttered. A list of these is given on the pages following.

A fourth way to build faith is to look at the faith of others—in particular, the great heroes of old that we read about in the scriptures. Why was Daniel willing to pray under threat of death? Or the young man David to battle the giant soldier Goliath? Or the disciples of Jesus to suffer the many persecutions even unto death? Were the hundreds or even thousands delusional, or was it rational choice?

God has given us sufficient evidence to believe that He is. Consequently, we make the choice to believe or disbelieve. If we say there is no God, we have no responsibility to Him. If we say that there is One who created us and sustains us and expects something from us, then that brings responsibilities. It requires not only belief *in* God, but also to *believe* God.

We must believe that Jesus is our Savior, the Son of God in order to become a follower of Christ (Mark 16:16), but this is only the beginning of the developing of our faith. The rest of our lives should be devoted to believing in God and believing God more and more. That is our goal for this month—to deepen and strengthen our belief.

Prophecies That Jesus Fulfilled

Prophecies Concerning His Birth	Prophecy	Fulfillment
Born of the seed of woman	Genesis 3:15	Galatians 4:4
Born of a virgin	Isaiah 7:14	Matthew 1:18; Matthew 1:24-25
Son of God	Psalm 2:7	Matthew 3:17
Seed of Abraham	Genesis 22:18	Matthew 1:1
Son of Isaac	Genesis 21:12	Luke 3:23; Luke 3:34
Tribe of Judah	Genesis 49:10	Luke 3:23; Luke 3:33
Family line of Jesse	Isaiah 11:1	Luke 3:23; Luke 3:32
House of David	Jeremiah 23:5	Luke 3:23; Luke 3:31
Born at Bethlehem	Micah 5:2	Matthew 2:1
Presented with gifts	Psalm 72:10	Matthew 2:1; Matthew 2:11
Herod kills children	Jeremiah 31:15	Matthew 2:16
Prophecies Concerning His Nature	**Prophecy**	**Fulfillment**
His pre-existence	Micah 5:2	Colossians 1:17; John 17:5
He shall be called Lord	Psalm 110:1	Matthew 22:43-45
Shall be immanuel	Isaiah 7:14	Matthew 1:23
Shall be a prophet	Deuteronomy 18:18	Matthew 21:11
Priest	Psalm 110:4	Hebrews 3:1
Judge	Isaiah 33:22	John 5:30
King	Psalm 2:6	Matthew 27:37
Special anointing of Holy Spirit	Isaiah 11:2	Matthew 3:16-17
His zeal for God	Psalm 69:9	John 2:15-16
Prophecies Concerning His Ministry	**Prophecy**	**Fulfillment**
Preceded by a messenger	Isaiah 40:3	Matthew 3:1-2
Ministry began in Galilee	Isaiah 9:1	Matthew 3:12
Ministry of miracles	Isaiah 35:5-6	Matthew 9:35
Teacher of parables	Psalm 78:2	Matthew 13:34
He was to enter the temple	Malachi 3:1	Matthew 21:12
He was to enter Jerusalem on a donkey	Zechariah 9:9	Luke 19:35-37
Stone of stumbling to Jews	Psalm 118:22	1 Peter 2:7
Light to Gentiles	Isaiah 60:3	Acts 13:47-48
Prophecies Concerning Events After His Burial	**Prophecy**	**Fulfillment**
Resurrection	Psalm 16:10	Acts 2:31
Ascension	Psalm 68:18	Acts 1:9
Session	Psalm 110:1	Hebrews 1:3

Prophecies Fulfilled in One Day	Prophecy	Fulfillment
Betrayed by a friend	Psalm 41:9	Matthew 10:4
Sold for 30 pieces of silver	Zechariah 11:12	Matthew 26:15
Money to be thrown into God's house	Zechariah 11:13	Matthew 27:5
Price given for potter's field	Zechariah 11:13	Matthew 27:7
Forsaken by His disciples	Zechariah 13:7	Mark 14:50
Accused by false witnesses	Psalm 35:11	Matthew 26:59-60
Silent before accusers	Isaiah 53:7	Matthew 27:12
Wounded and bruised	Isaiah 53:5	Matthew 27:26
Smitten and spit upon	Isaiah 50:6	Matthew 26:67
Mocked	Psalm 22:7-8	Matthew 27:29
Fell under the cross	Psalm 109:24-25	John 19:17
Hands and feet pierced	Psalm 22:16	Luke 23:33
Crucified with thieves	Isaiah 53:12	Matthew 27:38
Made intercession for His persecutors	Isaiah 53:12	Luke 23:34
Rejected by His own countrymen	Isaiah 53:3	John 7:5; John 7:48
Hated without a cause	Psalm 69:4	John 15:25
Friends stood afar off	Psalm 38:11	Luke 23:49
People shook their heads	Psalm 109:25	Matthew 27:39
Stared upon	Psalm 22:17	Luke 23:35
Garments parted and lots cast	Psalm 22:18	John 19:23-24
To suffer thirst	Psalm 69:21	John 19:28
Gall and vinegar offered to Him	Psalm 69:21	Matthew 27:34
His forsaken cry	Psalm 22:1	Matthew 27:46
Committed Himself to God	Psalm 31:5	Luke 23:46
Bones not broken	Psalm 34:20	John 19:33
Heartbroken	Psalm 22:14	John 19:34
His side pierced	Zechariah 12:10	John 19:34
Darkness over the land	Amos 8:9	Matthew 27:45
Buried in a rich man's tomb	Isaiah 53:9	Matthew 27:57-60

"We Saw Thee Not When Thou Didst Come"

We saw thee not when thou didst come
To this poor world of sin and death;
Nor yet beheld thy cottage home,
In that despised Nazareth;
But we believe thy footsteps trod
Its streets and plains, thou Son of God;
But we believe thy footsteps trod
Its streets and plains, thou Son of God.

We saw thee not when lifted high
Amid that wild and savage crew;
Nor heard we that imploring cry,
"Forgive, they know not what they do!"
But we believe the deed was done,
That shook the earth and veiled the sun;
But we believe the deed was done,
That shook the earth and veiled the sun.

We gazed not in the open tomb
Where once thy mangled body lay;
Nor saw thee in that "upper room,"
Nor met thee on the open way;
But we believe that angels said,
"Why seek the living with the dead?"
But we believe that angels said,
"Why seek the living with the dead?"

We walked not with the chosen few
Who saw thee from the earth ascend;
Who raised to heaven their wondering view,
Then low to earth all prostrate bend;
But we believe that human eyes
Beheld that journey to the skies;
But we believe that human eyes
Beheld that journey to the skies.

Then Jesus told him, "Because you have seen me, you have believed; blessed are those who have not seen and yet have believed" (John 20:29).

Believe That He Is: Class Preparation and Discussion

Class goals

- Increase our daily worship of God in praise and prayer
- Grow in grace and knowledge of God

Things to do

1. Find passages that give an attribute or description of God. Read them every day. Share them with your family or friends. Bring them to class. We will create a class list to keep and use in our worship of God.

   _____

   _____

   _____

2. Read Hebrews 11:6. What are the two things listed in this verse required to come to God? _____

   _____

3. Read Joshua 2.

   a. Who in this chapter demonstrates great belief in God? _____

   b. How was her belief obtained (vs 10-11)? _____

      _____

   c. How did she demonstrate her faith?_____

      _____

4. Choose another Bible character that is an example of great faith. Where can we read about him/her in the scriptures?_____

   _____

   a. How did the person demonstrate faith?_____

      _____

   b. How do we demonstrate our faith?_____

      _____

c. How do the scriptures say we obtain faith? Give scripture. _____

_____

d. Find all the passages that you can that say faith/belief is necessary.

_____

_____

_____

e. What is the difference between believing in God and believing God? Find a passage that demonstrates each. _____

_____

_____

_____

5. Study the reading in this lesson. Be ready to discuss in class.

6. Grow in grace and knowledge of God. "But grow in the grace and knowledge of our Lord and Savior Jesus Christ. To him be the glory both now and to the day of eternity. Amen" (2 Peter 3:18, ESV).

In this lesson our goal is to believe in God and to believe God more. It is easy to say, "I believe in God," but do we believe enough to have courage? To deprive ourselves of other things we might want? To spend time every day to love and serve God? You will use the Application page to work on this most important basis for our relationship with God.

Remember, study each day.

Believe That He Is: Daily Application

In order to come to God, to draw near to Him, we must believe that He is. With this lesson, our goal is to build faith. It is easy to say, "I believe in God," but do we believe enough to have courage? To deprive ourselves of other things we might want? To spend time every day to love and serve God? Is our weak faith the cause of many of our other difficulties? Do we have weak faith and not even realize it? Every day, list an example of someone from the scriptures who had amazing faith. Read about them. Do we have that kind of faith? Write the passage here where you read about them. Make notes of any thoughts you have that can help you have greater faith. Pray that your faith will give you courage to stand for God, just like Rahab's did. Read your bible and pray every day, and grow, grow, grow.

1. Sunday: _____

    _____

2. Monday: _____

    _____

3. Tuesday: _____

    _____

4. Wednesday: _____

    _____

5. Thursday: _____

    _____

6. Friday: _____

    _____

7. Saturday: _____

    _____

Diligently Seek Him

Diligently Seek Him: Reading

"...for he who comes to God must believe that He is and that He is a rewarder of those who seek Him" (Hebrews 11:6b).

In the last lesson we focused on the first of the requirements to come to God—believing that He is. In this lesson we will focus on the second—that He rewards those who seek Him. I believe the reward is that we will find Him, similar to the promise in Deuteronomy 4:29. Do we believe this promise— that if we seek him with our whole heart, we will find Him? Then that should motivate us to do just that.

Think of the things that we seek. When a child is missing, the nation is alerted through an Amber Alert so that as many as possible can seek the missing child. If it were one of our own, imagine how diligently we would seek him. What else, if you lost it today, would you seek frantically? How we seek what we treasure!

We also seek goals. Perhaps we set a goal to become a runner or to get a college degree or maybe to buy a new house. We diligently seek to attain these goals.

Understanding our seeking of these physical things can help us to understand how we need to seek God. If we are not diligently seeking God, we are diligently seeking self. We are living our lives for self. We may be members of the church. We may go to every service. But are we yearning for God? Do our hearts reach out to Him constantly? If we don't yearn for Him, then we need to examine our hearts—to set our hearts—as we will see in our study.

> But from there you will **seek** the Lord your God, and you **will find Him** if you search for Him with all your heart and all your soul.
>
> - Deuteronomy 4:29

As we do our study of *diligently seeking God* this month, you may be surprised how many scriptures contain the concept. Start with a concordance or a searchable Bible to find all the references. Examine each one. Study the context of who is saying it, to whom is it being said, and why. Write these things down. Make notes of anything that arouses interest or incites a question. Do your study *every day*.

If you find at the end of the day that you've been too busy to study, then you've been too busy. Our day is not over until we've studied our Bibles. "Every day without God is a bad day." Even if you are tired, gather your Bible and study for at least 15 minutes before you go to sleep. Then pray to God to praise Him and examine your day with Him. You'll be glad you did! Please don't say, "I'll catch up tomorrow," unless there is an extreme emergency. Nothing can make our lives richer than studying the word *every* day. If you get in this habit now, your life will be blessed. This is seeking Him, and if we do it with our whole hearts, He has promised that we will find Him.

> But **seek first** His kingdom and His righteousness, and all these things will be added to you.
>
> - Matthew 6:33

Once I took my husband to the hospital for a test that lasted several hours. While I was in the waiting room, I picked up one of the magazines lying there. Meanwhile, a young woman came in and sat down. She reached in her purse, pulled out a Bible and began to read. I felt so ashamed. Why hadn't I done that? I hadn't even thought of it. My heart was not where it should have been. Father, I want a heart that seeks You.

We have learned that if we want to draw near to God we must seek Him, and if we seek Him with our whole heart, we will find Him. On the other hand, if we are not seeking God, then we are seeking self. And in fact, we may be diligently seeking self.

SEEK GOD   OR   **SEEK SELF**

Why seek Him?

To rule over our life (Matthew 6:33).

For our strength (Ephesians 6:10).

To rely on (2 Corinthians 3:5).

To put our confidence in (2 Timothy 1:12).

To exalt Him (Psalm 34:3).

How to seek Him?

With whole heart.

When to seek Him?

Daily.

Sow a thought, reap an act.

Sow an act, reap a habit.

Sow a habit, reap a character.

Sow a character, reap your destiny.

So, **acts** become **habits** become **character**.

Purpose?

To God's glory and **to our good**.

A Biblical Example of Seeking God and Seeking Self: King Asa

For much of his life, King Asa, king of Judah, obeyed God. Asa did what was good and right in the eyes of the LORD. He removed the foreign altars and the high places, smashed the sacred stones and cut down the Asherah poles. He commanded Judah to seek the LORD and to obey his laws and commands. He removed the high places and incense altars in every town in Judah, and the kingdom was undisturbed under him (2 Chronicles 14:2-5).

These righteous deeds pleased God and as a consequence the nation enjoyed peace for ten years (verses 1, 6). But after this period of tranquility King Asa faced one of his most challenging tests. Zerah, the Ethiopian, led an immense army of one million men and three hundred chariots into Judah (verse 9). Asa cried out to God imploring Him for help. "Then Asa called to the LORD his God and said, 'LORD, there is no one like you to help the powerless against the mighty. Help us, O LORD our God, for we rely on you, and in your name we have come against this vast army. O LORD, you are our God; do not let man prevail against you'" (verse 11). The young king Asa trusted in God and His power. As a result God gave Judah a mighty victory (verse 13) along with a huge amount of plunder from cities all around their victory. So what appeared to be a potential disaster turned out to be a source of great prosperity.

After the battle, God sent His prophet Azariah to meet the victorious king to convey an important message. The prophet said, "The LORD is with you while you are with Him. If you seek Him, He will be found by you; but if you forsake Him He will forsake you" (2 Chronicles 15:2). The people responded with enthusiasm and confirmed their desire to follow the good example of their king. In chapter 15:10-12, we read: "They assembled at Jerusalem in the third month of the fifteenth year of Asa's reign. At that time they sacrificed to the LORD seven

> ...the Lord is **with you** when you are with Him. And if you **seek** Him, He will let you **find** Him; but if you **forsake** Him, He will forsake you.
>
> - 2 Chronicles 15:2

hundred head of cattle and seven thousand sheep and goats from the plunder they had brought back. They entered into a covenant to seek the LORD, the God of their fathers, with all their heart and soul." Judah and Asa then experienced more than 20 years of peace and prosperity.

But war threatened them again in the thirty-sixth year of Asa's reign. This time it was the northern kingdom of Israel that came against them. Rather than seeking God's help as he had before, Asa worked out his own plan. Asa took the silver and gold out of the treasuries of the Lord's temple and of his own palace and sent it to Ben-Hadad king of Aram, who was ruling in Damascus. "Let there be a treaty between me and you," he said, "as there was between my father and your father. See, I am sending you silver and gold. Now break your treaty with Baasha king of Israel so he will withdraw from me" (16:2, 3).

Asa's plan seemed to work. Ben Hadad went to war against the northern kingdom who ceased threatening Judah, but God was not pleased. Hanani, the seer, came to Asa king of Judah and said to him, "Because you relied on the king of Aram and not on the LORD your God, the army of the king of Aram has escaped from your hand. Were not the Cushites and Libyans a mighty army with great numbers of chariots and horsemen? Yet when you relied on the LORD, he delivered them into your hand. For the eyes of the LORD range throughout the earth to strengthen those whose hearts are fully committed to him. You have done a foolish thing, and from now on you will be at war" (16:7-9).

Asa was so enraged with the seer that he put him in prison and also brutally oppressed some of the people (16:10). Asa's disobedience caused his leadership to deteriorate. A once outstanding king became a great oppressor of the people because of his disobedience and pride. Sadly, Asa set himself on a course of judgment and an early death. In the thirty-ninth year of his reign, Asa was afflicted with a disease in his feet. Though his disease was severe, even in his illness he did not seek help from the Lord, but only from the physicians. Then in the forty-first year of his reign, Asa died and rested with his fathers (16:12, 13).

So a story that began so wonderfully ended in tragedy. A young leader who relied fully on the Lord ceased to seek Him. Remember his words as he sought God before he went to the early battle: "Help us, O LORD our God, for we rely on you." Let those be our words forever. We can know His will for us today through the word. We must seek it and follow it. This is the way that we rely on God today. As Jesus prayed to the Father, "Sanctify them through thy truth: thy word is truth: (John 17:17).

Diligently Seek Him: Class Preparation and Discussion

Class goals

- Increase our daily worship of God in praise and prayer
- Grow in grace and knowledge of God

Things to do

1. Find a passage that gives an attribute or description of God. Read it every day. Share it with your family or friends. Bring it to class. We will create a class list to keep and use in our worship of God.

    _____

    _____

    _____

2. Read Deuteronomy 4:29. This passage says to the children of Israel that they will find God if they do what? _____

    _____

3. Read Psalm 63. Why did David seek God? _____

    _____

4. Write down three other scriptures that talk about seeking God and any thoughts that you have from the reading. _____

    _____

    _____

    _____

5. Think of the Amber Alert. A child goes missing and the whole country goes on alert to seek the missing child. If it were our child, how diligent would we be in our search? Think of how this relates to our seeking of God. _____

    _____

6. Read 2 Chronicles 12:14. Why does this passage say that Rehoboam did evil? Are we like Rehoboam? _____

    _____

7. Study the readings in this lesson. Be ready to discuss in class.

8. Grow in grace and knowledge of God. "But grow in the grace and knowledge of our Lord and Savior Jesus Christ. To him be the glory both now and to the day of eternity. Amen" (2 Peter 3:18, ESV).

Drawing closer to God does not happen by accident. It only happens if we diligently seek Him. "Now set your mind and heart to seek the Lord your God" (1 Chronicles 22:19). This setting of the mind is the opposite of mental coasting. It is a conscious choice to direct the heart toward God. This is what Paul prays for the church: "May the Lord direct your hearts to the love of God and to the steadfastness of Christ" (2 Thessalonians 3:5). This month we will do an intense study from the scriptures about the concept of seeking God. Use the Application sheet to record your findings.

Remember, study each day.

Diligently Seek Him: Daily Application

This month we will study the concept of seeking God. These scriptures are given to help begin your study. Each day read the scripture. Write down any thoughts you have about the reading. Pray that you will diligently seek Him. Share with others what you read. Read your Bible and pray every day and grow, grow, grow.

1. Sunday: Read Deuteronomy 4:29. We will find God if we seek Him how? Pray for this. _____

2. Monday: Read Matthew 6:33. What should be our first priority in life? Reflection: of all the things that you seek in your life, is this first, i.e. of highest priority? I heard a preacher say once that it doesn't say what to seek second because it we don't seek this first, nothing else matters. And if we do, everything else will take care of itself._____
   _____

3. Tuesday: Read Matthew 6:33. God's righteousness is often called "behavior that pleases God." Find a verse that tells of a behavior that you need to work on to please God more. Seek it first today and every day. Pray to seek to please God with more righteous behavior.
   _____

4. Wednesday: Read Psalm 105:1-3. What should those who seek the Lord do in their heart? Pray to do this today._____
   _____

5. Thursday: Find a song that talks about seeking God. Worship Him in song today._____

6. Friday: Read Psalm 105:4 and Psalm 34:16. Thought question: When you seek the Lord's face, what are you seeking? Is it a literal "face"?
   _____

7. Saturday: Where is the idea of Psalm 34:16 repeated in the New Testament?_____

8. Sunday: This idea of seeking the Lord's face is repeated over and over in the Old Testament. Can you find other references? _____
   _____

9.   Monday: Read Revelation 22:4. When will we be able to fully see the face of God? Do you long for the time that God's face will be toward us and we can see it? _____

_____

10. Tuesday: Read Amos 5:14. What does Amos say to seek? What is the result if we do? _____

_____

11. Wednesday: Read Colossians 3:1. What are we to seek according to this verse? _____

_____

12. Thursday: Read 1 Peter 3:11. What are we to seek according to this verse?

_____

13. Friday: Read Proverbs 28:5. What are "those who seek the Lord" contrasted with in this verse? Ask yourself, which am I? _____

_____

14. Saturday: Read Philippians 2:21. What do these seek? Ask yourself if you do this. _____

15. Sunday: Read John 4:23. What does the Father seek? Do you want to be one of those that the Father seeks? _____

_____

16. Wednesday: Read 1 Peter 5:8. What is the devil seeking? Find the verse that says what to do to get the devil to flee from us. How hard are we resisting the devil today? Seeking God and resisting the devil go hand in hand. _____

_____

17. Thursday: Read Psalms 51. When we have sinned, what do we need to seek from God? _____

_____

18. Friday: Read 2 Chronicles 15:2. God makes two promises to Asa that are still true today. Which one do we desire? _____

_____

19. Saturday: Read the story of Asa in 2 Chronicles 14-17. Notice how Asa changed, first relying on God and seeking Him and later ignoring Him. This reminds me of our eagerness to seek God when we first become Christians, but it lessens later. Pray today to revive your seeking of Him. No spiritual coasting. Let's set our hearts on Him.

20. Sunday: Summarize your goal in seeking God. Let us pray that we will grow more and more to seek God, His kingdom, and His righteousness.

_____

_____

Love God With Your Whole Heart

Love God With Your Whole Heart: Reading

We read in Matthew 22 of a question posed by a Pharisee to Jesus, testing him: "Teacher, which is the great commandment in the Law?" Jesus answered in verse 37, "You shall love the Lord your God with all your heart, and with all your soul, and with all your mind. This is the great and foremost commandment."

Loving God with our whole being is a command. Why would we love God so much? 1 John 4:19 says, "We love Him because he first loved us." God's love motivates a reciprocal love for Him. He expressed His love in the sacrifice of His Son. So the answer to these questions is, we love Him because of what He has done for us. Do we doubt His great love in light of His great gift? Does it not deserve our own whole-hearted love?

Our love for God is an emotion, an action, and a commitment.

1. The *emotion* of love is our heart and mind recognizing His character and worshipping Him because of it. It is the awesome wonder that we experience when we consider all the worlds His hands have made. It is how we scarcely can take it in when we think that He did not spare his Son but sent Him to die. Those ideas from that great song "How Great Thou Art" express the emotion of love. Think of how many examples we have of David's love for God through worship. How wonderful it is to think of God every day, to worship Him privately in our hearts and to share with others. This is why we

> You shall **love** the Lord your God with all your **heart**, and with all your **soul**, and with all your **mind**. This is the great and foremost commandment.
>
> - Matthew 22:37

are studying His attributes, to know Him more and more.

2. The *action* of love for God is obedience, avoiding sin because of our love for Him.

   Joseph is a wonderful example of this. Read Genesis 39. Joseph was 17 years old when he was sold into slavery (Genesis 37:2). He was 30 when Pharaoh promoted him (Genesis 41:46) and had been in prison for two years before that (Genesis 41:1). So he was in Potiphar's house for 11 years, from approximately 17 to 28. Joseph's appearance was of special note. The Bible says Joseph was handsome in form and appearance. When Potiphar's wife repeatedly tried to seduce him to lie with her, note what he said: "How then can I do this great wickedness, and sin against God?" He refused to sin because he would not sin against God. That is the action of love.

> We **love** Him because he first **loved us**.
>
> - 1 John 4:19

3. The *commitment* of love towards God is perseverance, never giving up on our relationship with Him. Because we love God, we won't give up our relationship.

   The apostle Paul is a great example of this form of love. Think of all he endured. "We are hard pressed on every side, but not crushed; perplexed, but not in despair; persecuted, but not abandoned; struck down, but not destroyed" (2 Corinthians 4 8). He didn't let persecution crush him. He didn't let it send him into despair. He was persecuted but not abandoned by God. And even though he was struck down, he didn't let it destroy him. He didn't forsake His God.

Consider the lyrics of this great old hymn. Do you see the three components of love in the song?

"My Jesus I Love Thee"

My Jesus, I love Thee, I know Thou art mine;
For Thee all the follies of sin I resign.
My gracious Redeemer, my Savior art Thou;
If ever I loved Thee, my Jesus, 'tis now.

I love Thee because Thou has first loved me,
And purchased my pardon on Calvary's tree.
I love Thee for wearing the thorns on Thy brow;
If ever I loved Thee, my Jesus, 'tis now.

I'll love Thee in life, I will love Thee in death,
And praise Thee as long as Thou lendest me breath;
And say when the death dew lies cold on my brow,
If ever I loved Thee, my Jesus, 'tis now.

In mansions of glory and endless delight,
I'll ever adore Thee in heaven so bright;
I'll sing with the glittering crown on my brow;
If ever I loved Thee, my Jesus, 'tis now.

We can work to love God more and more every day. If we reflect on His love and His goodness every day, we can learn to love "with all our heart, and with all our soul, and with all our mind." With all our everything. The more we love God, the closer to Him we will be. Let's make that our goal this month.

Love God With Your Whole Heart: Class Preparation and Discussion

Class goals

- Increase our daily worship of God in praise and prayer
- Grow in grace and knowledge of God

Things to do

1. Find a passage that gives an attribute or description of God. Read it every day. Share it with your family or friends. Bring it to class. We will create a class list to keep and use in our worship of God.

    _____

    _____

    _____

2. Read Matthew 22:37.

    a. Write down three other scriptures that tell us to love God._____

    _____

    b. Was it important to God that early peoples loved Him? What is the first verse that we find in the scriptures that tells us to love God?

    _____

3. Give an example of someone from the scriptures that you would say loved the Lord whole-heartedly. Where can we find it in the scriptures? What is the evidence that he/she loved God wholeheartedly?_____

    _____

    _____

4. Read Romans 5:8 and 1 John 4:19.

    a. How did God demonstrate His love for us?_____

    _____

    b. From 1 John, 4:19, we love God, because _____

    _____

    c.   Name one way we can demonstrate our love for God. _____

_____

5.   Study the lesson readings.

6.   Grow in grace and knowledge of God. "But grow in the grace and knowledge of our Lord and Savior Jesus Christ. To him be the glory both now and to the day of eternity. Amen" (2 Peter 3:18, ESV).

Love in all its forms is the centerpiece of the scriptures—God's love for us, our love for Him, and our love for others. Our love for God will motivate us to draw near to Him; hence we should focus more and more on building our love. Our goal this lesson is to increase our love for God. Use the next page to recognize the characteristics of God that will cause us to love Him more and more.

Remember, study each day.

Love God With Your Whole Heart: Daily Application

God is love and we need to love Him in return. In Psalm 116:1, the psalmist says, "I love the LORD, because..." and then lists reasons that he loves Him. Each day, write an attribute or act of God that causes you to love Him. *Include the scripture* where it is found. Search your heart and make it something that really means a lot to you. Make this a prayer to God. Many hymns recognize our love for God. *Write the song lyrics* and have the song in your heart throughout the day. After the Psalmist said he loved God for what God had done, then he said, "so I will call on Him as long as I live." Do we love God enough to seek Him, to obey Him, to devote more and more of our lives and time to Him? Think of your emotion of love, acts of love, and commitment of love for God.

1. Sunday: I love God because _____

_____

2. Monday: I love God because _____

_____

3. Tuesday: I love God because _____

_____

4. Wednesday: I love God because _____

_____

5. Thursday: I love God because_____

_____

6. Friday: I love God because _____

_____

7. Saturday: I love God because _____

_____

Love God by Loving Others

Love God by Loving Others: Reading

We cannot seek God or love God without loving others. When someone asked Jesus what was the most important part of the Law of Moses, He said, "You shall love the Lord your God with all your heart, with all your soul, and with all your mind. This is the first and great commandment. And the second is like it: You shall love your neighbor as yourself. On these two commandments hang all the Law and the Prophets" (Matthew 22:37-40).

God is love. He has done so much for us that we want to return that love, but how? One very important way is to love others. In fact, Jesus says that when we serve others, we serve Him, and when we fail to serve others, we fail to serve Him (Matthew 25:31-46). In this scene, the people ask, "When did we see you hungry?" It is as if they are saying, "Jesus, we would have served *you*. If *you'd* been there, Jesus, we'd have served *you*." But Jesus is pointing out that we serve Him by serving others—and not just others, but the least of others. The least of others may be an older lady from the congregation in a nursing home. The least of others may be someone who annoys us but needs our love. The least of others may be an elderly lady that needs someone to give her attention at church services or through a card. We all have "the least of others" in our lives that Jesus expects us to love if we love Him.

Many scriptures tell us how to love and serve others. 1 Corinthians 13 is, of course, the "love chapter." We probably know what the love behaviors are, but sometimes we don't look for the

> You shall **love the Lord** your God with all your heart, with all your soul, and with all your mind. This is the first and great commandment. And the second is like it: You shall **love your neighbor** as yourself.
>
> - Matthew 22:37-39

opportunity to express them. We are too focused on ourselves and what *we* want.

In this lesson we will focus every day on loving God by loving others. Plan to do a small kindly deed for others every day. Not just for this month but for a lifetime. Remember, acts become habits, and habits become character. Offer your "cup of cold water" to someone in the name of God. Remember this song?

There is Room in the Kingdom

Just a cup of cold water in His name given
May the hope in some heart renew;
Do not wait to be told, nor by sorrow driven
To the work God has planned for you.

Wake up every day saying, "Who can I serve today? Who needs my help today?" Serve God by serving others. Love God by loving others.

In class we want to have a good discussion about whether we will have a servant's heart to help others. It is what God expects of us, but it doesn't happen by accident. It doesn't have to be a big, huge deal either. It may just be a smile and a hello to older ladies in the congregation. Every Sunday morning just say, "I am going to smile and say hello to a widow lady today." It could be a card or a hug to someone who needs encouraging. Tell someone how much you appreciate them. Tell a young man that reads the scripture that he did a good job. It may be a visit to the nursing home or food taken to the sick. But whatever it is, we need to learn to cultivate a daily habit of saying this prayer to God: "What can I do to love you today through loving others?" Then find that thing, do it, and give God the glory. As mothers, we serve God by serving our families, but at times we need to reach out and help others.

Who is a better example of loving God by loving others than Dorcas?

Be **kind to one another**, tenderhearted, forgiving one another, as God in Christ forgave you.

- Ephesians 4:32

In Joppa there was a disciple named Tabitha (in Greek her name is Dorcas); she was always doing good and helping the poor. About that time she became sick and died, and her body was washed and placed in an upstairs room. Lydda was near Joppa; so when the disciples heard that Peter was in Lydda, they sent two men to him and urged him, "Please come at once!"

Peter went with them, and when he arrived he was taken upstairs to the room. All the widows stood around him, crying and showing him the robes and other clothing that Dorcas had made while she was still with them.

Peter sent them all out of the room; then he got down on his knees and prayed. Turning toward the dead woman, he said, "Tabitha, get up." She opened her eyes, and seeing Peter she sat up. He took her by the hand and helped her to her feet. Then he called for the believers, especially the widows, and presented her to them alive. This became known all over Joppa, and many people believed in the Lord. (Acts 9:36-43, NIV)

In the same way that we look at love for God as emotion, action, and commitment, our love for others can be thought of in these same three ways.

The emotion of love for others is expressed in Ephesians 4:32. Paul instructs us to "Be kind to one another, tenderhearted, forgiving one another, as God in Christ forgave you." Being kind and compassionate means doing whatever is beneficial and benevolent to others. Forgiving one another is extending grace, treating others as Christ treats us.

Who is grating on you right now? How can you extend Christ's love to that person by "bearing with" him/her and place his/her interests ahead your own? This leads us to the actions of love.

1. Bear with one another. "With all humility and gentleness, with patience, bearing with one another in love" (Ephesians 4:2). In the last verse, "bearing with" one another is literally "to hold up, bear with, put up with," either in relationships or circumstances. In the context of Ephesians 4:2, the Word points us to four qualities that are needed to "bear with" one

> With all humility and gentleness, with patience, **bearing with one another in love**.
>
> - Ephesians 4:2

another: in humility, gentleness, patience, and love. Our natural tendency is to be provoked by others especially when they do not share our ideas or convictions. When we cling to our desires rather than the well being of others, we do not love God.

2. Serve one another through love. "For you were called to freedom, brothers. Only do not use your freedom as an opportunity for the flesh, but through love serve one another" (Galatians 5:13).

3. Encourage one another. "But encourage one another day after day, as long as it is still called 'today,' so that none of you will be hardened by the deceitfulness of sin" (Hebrews 3:13). "Therefore encourage one another and build one another up, just as you are doing" (1 Thessalonians 5:11).

4. Submit to one another (opposite of self-willed). "Submitting to one another out of reverence for Christ" (Ephesians 5:21). "Do nothing from selfish ambition or conceit, but in humility count others more significant than yourselves" (Philippians 2:3).

5. Forgiving one another. "Bearing with one another and, if one has a complaint against another, forgiving each other; as the Lord has forgiven you, so you also must forgive" (Colossians 3:13).

6. Seek to do good for one another. "See that no one repays anyone evil for evil, but always seek to do good to one another and to everyone" (1 Thessalonians 5:15).

Love for others as commitment—love never fails. "Bears all things, believes all things, hopes all things, endures all things. Love never fails" (1 Corinthians 13:7-8a). If we love others, we won't give up on our relationship with them. Jesus was conveying this when he answered the apostles to forgive seventy times seven times (Matthew 18:22). He was using this to represent forgiving as many times as you needed to.

When I think of what loving God through loving others means, I think of my children when they were small. They would sometimes color a picture and bring it to me with love as a gift. Or maybe they would pick a dandelion and bring it to mommy. Think of it, what could a tiny child give to their parents? Everything that they have comes from their parents. But this gift of love, as "worthless" as it is in silver or gold, brings joy to the parent's heart. It must be similar to our gifts that we give to God, our gifts of service. We have nothing of material value that we could give God that He needs. But I imagine Him accepting the gifts of our service in the same way as a mother accepts the gifts of her children.

Do you want to love God? Then let us love God by loving others. And that love must get out of our hearts and into our actions.

Love God by Loving Others: Class Preparation and Discussion

Class goals

- Increase our daily worship of God in praise and prayer
- Grow in grace and knowledge of God

Things to do

1. Find a passage that tells us something that we should do to please God. We will make a class list._____

    _____

2. Read 1 John 4:12, 20 at least once every day. Read it to your family and discuss it with at least one other person.

3. Write down three other scriptures that tell us to love one another.

    _____

4. Write three ways that we can show love to others in this congregation.

    _____

    _____

5. Read 1 Timothy 5:1-2. Think about how this passage relates to our relationships in the church. How can we serve other Christians?

    _____

6. Read Ephesians 4:32. What are the three things that we are told to do in this verse? _____

    _____

7. Name three things that Jesus did that showed an attitude of service?

    _____

    _____

8. Study the readings from this chapter. Be ready to discuss in class.

9. Grow in grace and knowledge of God. "But grow in the grace and knowledge of our Lord and Savior Jesus Christ. To him be the glory both now and to the day of eternity. Amen" (2 Peter 3:18, ESV).

Our goal this month is to show love towards others in this congregation with kind deeds. It does not happen automatically. We must pray, read our Bibles, and set our minds on kind and good deeds.

Remember, study each day.

Love God by Loving Others: Daily Application

Our goal this lesson is to show more love to others in the congregation. Every day ask the questions: Who needs me today? Who can I help today? Remember working daily helps us to turn acts into habits and habits into character. Who is your "least of others" that you need to help?

Describe how you work on it each day and how you succeeded or struggled. You will not need to share this in class. This is not a brag sheet. It is for you and your spiritual growth in serving others.

1. Sunday: _____
    _____
    _____

2. Monday: _____
    _____
    _____

3. Tuesday: _____
    _____
    _____

4. Wednesday: _____
    _____
    _____

5. Thursday: _____
    _____
    _____

6. Friday: _____
    _____
    _____

7. Saturday: _____
    _____
    _____

Love God by Obeying Him

Love God by Obeying Him: Reading

Jesus put it very clearly, "If you love me, you will keep my commandments" (John 14:15). He said it another way: "And why call ye me, Lord, Lord, and do not the things which I say?" (Luke 6:46). Our love for God and for His Son Jesus carries with it the responsibility of obedience.

We have studied the connection of belief and obedience, and those are clearly connected. I believe that God is, and I know that I have a responsibility to obey Him. But this passage gives us another, even higher connection with obedience. Not only do I believe Him, I love Him. Not only do I have a mental acceptance, I have an emotional reaction to God. I love Him. And that causes me to obey Him. And when I fail to obey Him, I have to admit that my love has failed. Because Jesus said, if you love me, you'll keep my commandments.

> And why call ye me, Lord, Lord, and **do not** the things which I **say**?
>
> - Luke 6:46

Who could give us a greater example of this responsibility of obedience than Joseph? "But he refused and said to his master's wife, 'Look, my master does not know what is with me in the house, and he has committed all that he has to my hand. There is no one greater in this house than I, nor has he kept back anything from me but you, because you are his wife. How then can I do this great wickedness, and sin against God?'" (Genesis 39:8-9).

How can I do this great wickedness, and sin against God? Have you ever thought those thoughts? Asked yourself that question? As we draw nearer to God, won't we judge sin in this way more and more? As we draw nearer to God, won't it break our hearts to know that we have let down God? Because if we love God, we will keep his commandments.

Self is a roadblock to our demonstration of our love for God through obedience. We live in a self-centered world where self is exalted and indulged, but self-denial, putting God's will before our own, is the real challenge. I won't do this act because I love God. That should become our daily thought. Or likewise, I *will* do this act because I love God.

If we love God as unselfishly as we should, we'll put obedience paramount in our hearts. It is easy to say the words, "I love you, Lord," but if we love Him, we will subject our will to His. That is the hard part, isn't it?

Remember the hymn, "My Jesus, I Love Thee":

My Jesus, I love Thee, I know Thou art mine;
For Thee all the follies of sin I resign;
My gracious Redeemer, my Savior art Thou;
If ever I loved Thee, my Jesus, 'tis now.

Love God by Obeying Him: Class Preparation and Discussion

Class goals

- Increase our daily worship of God in praise and prayer
- Grow in grace and knowledge of God

Things to do

1. Find a passage that tells us something that we should do to please God. We will make a class list.

   _____

   _____

   _____

2. Read John 14:15, 23-24 and answer the following questions.

   a. If I don't obey God, what is the logical conclusion from this passage?

      _____

   b. What are challenges to obeying God? Do we always obey? Where in the scriptures does it say that all have sinned? _____

      _____

      _____

   c. What should I do when I find that I have sinned? Where do I learn this? _____

   d. Christians help one another avoid sin. Match these resources that help keep us from sin.

      _____ Encouraging one another in the assemblies

      _____ Confess our faults one to another

      _____ Carry others' burdens

      _____ Encourage and build each other up

      1. James 5:16

      2. 1 Thessalonians 5:11

      3. Hebrews 10:24

      4. Galatians 6:2

3.   Read Romans 12:21. Read it to your family and discuss it with at least one other person. Memorize the verse.

   a.   Who is someone in the scriptures that you would say was overcome with evil? Who is someone that you would say overcame evil with good? _____

   _____

   b.   How can we overcome evil with good? _____

   _____

4.   Read Psalm 34:18. Drawing nearer to God is the focus of this study.

   What separates us from God? _____

   What does David mean here by someone with a broken heart?_____

   _____

   What is a contrite heart? _____

5.   Study the lesson reading.

6.   Grow in grace and knowledge of God. Sometimes we go through our daily lives and don't reflect on whether we are obeying God that day. Obedience is not just avoiding sin, but also choosing to do righteous deeds. Reflect each day on our obedience and in our prayers seek strength to overcome. Use the Application sheet.

Remember, study each day.

Love God by Obeying Him: Daily Application

This month I want to be more aware of my obedience to God. I don't want to float through life, but each day I will reflect about my weaknesses that day and pray to overcome them. Did you face temptation that day? To be unkind? To be selfish? To be unforgiving? Sometimes we fail to see these sins of the heart as disobedience. Do a study of a contrite heart. Are we as sorry as we should be when we are not as obedient as we should be? *Write a passage* each day that helps you focus on your full obedience to God.

Describe how you work on it each day and how you succeeded or struggled.

1. Sunday: _____
   _____
   _____

2. Monday: _____
   _____
   _____

3. Tuesday: _____
   _____
   _____

4. Wednesday: _____
   _____
   _____

5. Thursday: _____
   _____
   _____

6. Friday: _____
   _____
   _____

7. Saturday: _____
   _____
   _____

God Provides Victory Over Life's Problems

God Provides Victory Over Life's Problems: Reading

This will come as no surprise to anyone—life is not always easy, even for Christians. It certainly wasn't easy for the Apostle Paul. "Five different times the Jewish leaders gave me thirty-nine lashes. Three times I was beaten with rods. Once I was stoned. Three times I was shipwrecked. Once I spent a whole night and a day adrift at sea. I have traveled on many long journeys. I have faced danger from rivers and from robbers. I have faced danger from my own people, the Jews, as well as from the Gentiles. I have faced danger in the cities, in the deserts, and on the seas. And I have faced danger from men who claim to be believers but are not. I have worked hard and long, enduring many sleepless nights. I have been hungry and thirsty and have often gone without food. I have shivered in the cold, without enough clothing to keep me warm" (2 Corinthians 11; 24-27).

How could he possibly endure all that? And not only endure, but overcome, conquer? In today's vernacular, we would say Paul was a survivor. It's the idea that hard times can't get us down. Hit me with your best shot. I will survive. But how? How did Paul do it, and how can we?

The God that made us and loves us certainly recognizes the hardships of life. He has promised to provide us with what we need to overcome. Consider these promises.

> What then shall we say to these things? If God is for us, who can be against us? He who did not spare His own Son, but delivered Him up for us all, how shall

Rejoice in the Lord always; again I will say, **rejoice**!

- Philippians 4:4

He not with Him also freely give us all things? Who shall bring a charge against God's elect? It is God who justifies. Who is he who condemns? It is Christ who died, and furthermore is also risen, who is even at the right hand of God, who also makes intercession for us. Who shall separate us from the love of Christ? Shall tribulation, or distress, or persecution, or famine, or nakedness, or peril, or sword? As it is written: "For Your sake we are killed all day long; We are accounted as sheep for the slaughter." Yet in all these things we are more than conquerors through Him who loved us. For I am persuaded that neither death nor life, nor angels nor principalities nor powers, nor things present nor things to come, nor height nor depth, nor any other created thing, shall be able to separate us from the love of God which is in Christ Jesus our Lord. (Romans 8:31-39)

We need to read that over and over, because hard times are going to come—illness, loneliness, loss of a job, physical or emotional abuse, financial burdens, loss of a loved one, and temptations are just a few of the personal struggles that we might face. Yet God has promised us that we won't be just conquerors, we'll be *more than* conquerors. We can *more than* conquer the problems that confront us. Like Paul, we can conquer with joy. "Rejoice in the Lord always; again I will say, rejoice!" (Philippians 4:4).

This verse is not always understood. It does not mean that Christians should never feel sadness or grief. We know Jesus wept at Lazarus' death. And Paul wrote in Romans 9:2 that, "I have great sorrow and continual grief in my heart."

Rejoice in the Lord always, and again I say rejoice. It is a twice-stated command that we must choose to obey, deliberately and purposely. As a mother, I think of the loss of a child or grandchild. What could be more devastating? Of course, I would not rejoice over that. I would not rejoice in the loss of my child. But I can rejoice in the Lord at that time. The Lord is great cause for rejoicing in all circumstances, even if I might be weeping over my loss or someone else's loss. What does Romans 12:15 say?

It has to do with our faith. Do we trust God when He says that if He is for us, who can be against us? Then that is great cause for rejoicing in the Lord, even if we are heartbroken over a loss. Do we believe that nothing can separate us from the love of God, no trials, no unfair treatment, no disappointment, no circumstances, no illness, no death of a loved one? Nothing? Then that is cause for rejoicing in the Lord. We may feel grief. We may feel sadness or disappointment, but we rejoice in the Lord because we know that God has made promises to us that He will fulfill. And that is cause for great rejoicing in the Lord. And it is victory.

When we are in anguish, we can remember, "Do not sorrow, for the joy of the Lord is your strength" (Nehemiah 8:10).

God Provides Victory Over Life's Problems: Class Preparation and Discussion

Class goals

- Increase our daily worship of God in praise and prayer
- Grow in grace and knowledge of God

Things to do

1. Find a passage that tells us something that we should do to please God. Read it to your family and discuss it with at least one other person.

    _____

    _____

    _____

2. Read 2 Timothy 4:16-17. What challenge was Paul experiencing? How did he withstand it?_____

    _____

3. Read 1 John 5:4. What is the victory that overcomes the world? _____

4. Of whom was Satan speaking when Satan claimed that the person worshipped God just because God was so good to him? _____
    Passage? _____ What problems did God allow Satan to place upon him?_____
    How did he show victory over those problems?_____

    _____

5. Name three problems that women face today (this may not be you personally, but things that you may see others facing). _____

    _____

    _____

6. Read Psalms 46:1-3.

    a. Why did David say he would not fear? _____

        _____

  b.   He would not fear, even if what happened? _____

_____

7.   Find the passage that says, "if God is for us, who can be against us."

_____

8.   Study the lesson reading. Be ready to discuss in class.

9.   Grow in grace and knowledge of God. Every day this month, we want to focus on God's presence as a means to overcome our problems. We have focused on growing our love for God, on seeking Him, and on increasing our faith. We are now putting all of that into practice as we think of how God gives us victory over life's problems.

Remember, study each day.

God Provides Victory Over Life's Problems: Daily Application

Each day this month we will read a passage that shows how faith in our great God can give us strength to overcome life's problems. Our problems may feel minor at this time. We are blessed. Or they may feel major. We are still blessed even though it may be harder to realize it. Regardless of our current situation, we need to prepare our hearts and build our faith so that when problems come, we are prepared.

1. Sunday: 2 Samuel 22:33

2. Monday: Psalm 33:20

3. Tuesday: Psalm 46:1-2

4. Wednesday: Philippians 4:6-7

5. Thursday: Isaiah 40:31

6. Friday: Ephesians 3:20-21

7. Saturday: Philippians 4:13

Challenges for Christian Women

Challenges for Christian Women: Reading

Closeness to God requires a continual guarding against sin. "Brethren, if a man is overtaken in any trespass, you who are spiritual restore such a one in a spirit of gentleness, considering yourself lest you also be tempted" (Galatians 6:1). The second part of this verse is a sobering warning. And this warning is given to those who are "spiritual." He isn't saying, you weak Christians can be tempted. He is saying, be careful spiritual Christians that you aren't tempted. The warning is given another way in 1 Corinthians 10:12: "Therefore let him who thinks he stands take heed lest he fall."

Temptation is not a sin. It is a sign that blinks "Danger! Danger ahead." Don't go there. Not another step. Turn and run because there is something terrible ahead. Seldom do Christians jump into sin with one giant leap. We see the temptation, we get a step closer and closer. For instance, imagine a woman and man who work together. They find each other fun to be with, so they go to lunch together by themselves. What could be wrong with that? It's just lunch. This may never turn into sin. It may stop right there. But surely we can see that there is potential for danger there. And it seems a good time to say, "you that think you stand, take heed lest you fall."

We know the passage "for all have sinned and fall short of the glory of God," (Romans 3:23), and "If we say that we have no sin, we deceive ourselves, and the truth is not in us" (1 John 1:8). That includes us, doesn't it? Me, you, everyone in this class, the

> Brethren, if a man is overtaken in any **trespass**, you who are **spiritual** restore such a one in a spirit of gentleness, **considering yourself** lest you also be tempted.
>
> - Galatians 6:1

preacher and the elders. It includes even David (the man after God's own heart) with Bathsheba, even the great leader Moses when he struck the rock and even the apostle Peter who vehemently claimed he would never deny Christ. So we must never say, "Not me, I would never do that."

Neither should we use this aspect of sin to minimize its importance, to shrug our shoulders and say to ourselves, "No big deal, everyone does it." How important is sin? So important to God that it cost Him the death of His Son. We must be careful not to think, "Oh, that's not so bad." "I'm just that way." "I have no patience." "I get angry and seek to fight back." "That's just the way I am." Remember the publican who would not so much as lift his head, but said, "God be merciful to me the sinner." And the Pharisee who was saying, "I'm not so bad. I'm pretty good, really. Nothing like him."

What challenges our nearness to God? Satan uses many things to draw us away from God. A few common ones include:

The media. The world comes into our lives through our phones, tv, etc. Surely we can see what a negative influence that can have on us, especially on our young people. Parents must use judgment and wisdom about what is best for their children and for their family's welfare in this regard. Parents, be strong to stand up for what you believe is right. This may be the biggest threat to our children's relationship with God.

Busyness. We are challenged by a "busyness" that keeps us from spending the time that we should on our family's spiritual lives. When I was a young woman, I can remember that futurists predicted that computers were going to make it so that people had so much time on their hands, that we wouldn't know what to do with it. They said that a huge leisure industry would spring up to help us fill the many hours that we would have on our hands. WRONG! People in our culture are so busy that they are often stressed and don't devote their lives to God as they should. When I taught high school, I saw many, many young people who came to school exhausted from lack of sleep. Sometimes children are into so many extra-curricular activities that the family spends little time together. Or the husband and father works such long hours that he seldom has time to lead the family properly. And the wife and mother works, so she rushes through her work at home in a frazzled and over-wrought way. Perhaps your family is not as extreme as I've described here, but examine your family busy-ness to see if it is pulling you away from God.

We are challenged by selfishness that motivates us to please ourselves rather than God or others. Perhaps nothing can rob us of our walk with God like selfishness. Philippians 2:3-4 says, "Do nothing from rivalry or conceit, but in humility count others more significant than yourselves. Let each of you look not only to his own interests, but also to the interests of others." Think of how Abram was unselfish with Lot, giving him first choice of land. Think of how Joseph treated his brothers after all they had done to him. Of course, Jesus is our perfect example of unselfishness. Matthew 20:28 says, "Even as the Son of Man came not to be served but to serve, and to give his life as a ransom for many." Christ's example of His sacrifice for us is the ultimate unselfish act. What a challenge it is to us to put God and others before self.

All of our challenges can be overcome. God expects us to avoid sin. He also wants us to return to him when we sin. We don't overcome our challenges by just shrugging our shoulders and saying, "Oh well, this is how I am." Thoughts become actions. Actions become habits. Habits become character. We act today to look into our hearts to identify our weakness. We start with a contrite prayer of forgiveness. We act every day that God gives us. We pray and act, more and more, every day. Examine your own life to see what your challenges are. Then search God's word for the way to overcome them. Read the ten scriptures on the next page to find specific ways that we can overcome challenges. And ACT!

Challenges for Christian Women: Worksheet

How God provides victory and helps us to overcome our challenges!

Match scripture with principle.

_____ 1.   Remember the source of your joy.

_____ 2.   Examine your thoughts, refocus if necessary.

_____ 3.   Count your blessings.

_____ 4.   Make and work towards goals to grow closer to God.

_____ 5.   Smile and laugh.

_____ 6.   Do kindness for others.

_____ 7.   Take time to be sad when you need to be sad.

_____ 8.   Forgive others and forgive yourself.

_____ 9.   Develop healthy relationships.

_____ 10.   Have the right priorities.

Ecclesiastes 4:9–10a

Phillipians 4:8-9,

2 Peter 3:18

Proverbs 17:22

Matthew 25:40

Matthew 6:33

Ecclesiastes 3:4

Ephesians 4:31- 32

James 1:17

Colossians 3:15

God Provides Victory Over Life's Problems: Class Preparation and Discussion

Class goals

- Increase our daily worship of God in praise and prayer
- Grow in grace and knowledge of God

Things to do

1. Find a passage that tells us something that we should do to please God. We will make a class list.

   _____

   _____

   _____

2. Read Colossians 3:1-2. Read it to your family and discuss it with at least one other person.

3. What are earthly things that compete for *your* time, drawing your attention away from God? _____

   _____

4. Make a list of items that are tempting women today. _____

   _____

   _____

5. Read Matthew 26:41 What was the setting of this verse? What did Jesus say could guard against temptation? _____

   _____

6. Prepare the worksheet to see how God helps us to overcome our problems and challenges.

7. Study the lesson reading. Be ready to discuss.

8. Application: Each day this month we will reflect on challenges that women face in the world today. Each day, write one temptation that you know that women face, and list a scripture that would help overcome that challenge.

Remember, study each day.

Challenges for Christian Women: Daily Application

Each day this month we will reflect on challenges that women face in the world today. Each day, write one temptation that you know that women face, and list a scripture that would help overcome that challenge. Example: *Drinking*. Proverbs 20:1: "Wine is a mocker, strong drink is raging: and whosoever is deceived thereby is not wise." Consider which ones you face and pray to overcome. Don't forget sins of the heart like unforgiveness, etc.

1. Sunday: _____
   _____
   _____

2. Monday: _____
   _____
   _____

3. Tuesday: _____
   _____
   _____

4. Wednesday: _____
   _____
   _____

5. Thursday: _____
   _____
   _____

6. Friday: _____
   _____
   _____

7. Saturday: _____
   _____
   _____

"Every day without God is a bad day!"

Lesson 9

Godly Women

Godly Women: Reading

Deborah

Deborah is a woman of the Old Testament whose life teaches us some valuable lessons. We read about her in Judges 4 and 5.

After Judge Ehud died, the people did evil. The Lord then sold them into the hand of Jabin, king of Caanan. Sisera was head of Caanan's army. The Israelites were harshly oppressed by them for 20 years. They cried out to the Lord for deliverance (4:1-3).

Deborah was a prophetess, wife, and judge of Israel who the people came to for judgment. Feminists try to use Deborah as justification for women being leaders in the church today. But not everything that was allowed in the Old Testament is an example of what God wants for today. The New Testament directs us today. Below are just a few NT scriptures that indicate the role of women in the church today (4:4-5).

- 1 Timothy 2:11-12: Women are to learn in quietness and in subjection.

- 1 Corinthians 14:34-35: Women are not to speak in public worship assembly, as God's law places women under the leadership of man.

- 1 Timothy 3:1-12: She cannot be an elder or deacon, as one of the criteria is that they must be the husband of one wife. "If a man desires the office of a bishop, he desires a good work" (verse 1).

So what can women of today learn from Deborah? What are the lessons for us? To determine that, let's look at four statements that Deborah made and their application on our lives today.

> A woman must **quietly** receive instruction with entire **submissiveness**.
>
> - 1 Timothy 2:11

Deborah's statement 1: "Has not the Lord God of Israel commanded?" (Judges 4:6-7)

Lesson for us: We should strive to learn and obey God's commands. Deborah was guided without reservation by what God commanded and so must we.

- John 14:15-31: "If ye love me, keep my commandments."

- John 15:10: "If you keep My commandments, you will abide in My love; just as I have kept My Father's commandments and abide in His love."

- John 15:12: "This is My commandment, that you love one another, just as I have loved you."

- John 15:14: "You are My friends if you do what I command you."

- John 15:17: "This I command you, that you love one another."

Deborah's statement 2: "I will surely go with you..." (Judges 4:9)

Lesson for us: Faith in God gives us the courage to be strong. Think of how much courage it would have taken to agree to go into battle against this great army. Clearly, Deborah's faith gave her this courage.

- Joshua 1:9: "Have not I commanded thee? Be strong and of a good courage; be not afraid, neither be thou dismayed: for the LORD thy God is with thee whithersoever thou goest."

- Psalm 31:24: "Be of good courage, and he shall strengthen your heart, all ye that hope in the LORD."

- Acts 4:29: "And now, Lord, look upon their threats and grant to your servants to continue to speak your word with all boldness."

Deborah's statement 3: "Up! This is the day that the Lord God has delivered..." (Judges 4:14)

Lesson for us: Get to work. Deborah did not delay going to this great work. Likewise, we must be about our work for the Lord.

You are My **friends** if you do what I **command** you.

- John 15:14

- 1 Corinthians 15:58: "Therefore, my beloved brethren, be steadfast, immovable, always abounding in the work of the Lord, knowing that your toil is not in vain in the Lord."

- Matthew 25:40: "And the King shall answer and say unto them, Verily I say unto you, Inasmuch as ye have done it unto one of the least of these my brethren, ye have done it unto me."

- Matthew 25:45: "Then shall he answer them, saying, Verily I say unto you, Inasmuch as ye did it not to one of the least of these, ye did it not to me."

Deborah's statement 4: "I will sing praise to the Lord." (Judges 5:3)

Lesson for us: Give praise and thanksgiving for the victories of life. Deborah recognized that the victory was from the Lord, and she gave Him praise and thanksgiving. We must do likewise.

- 1 Peter 2:9: "But you are a chosen people, a royal priesthood, a holy nation, a people belonging to God, that you may declare the praises of him who called you out of darkness into his wonderful light."

- Psalm 69:30: "I will praise the name of God with song, And shall magnify Him with thanksgiving."

- Psalm 119:7: "I will praise you with an upright heart as I learn your righteous laws."

- Psalm 119:12: "Praise be to you, O LORD; teach me your decrees."

- 1 Timothy 1:17: "Now to the King eternal, immortal, invisible, the only God, be honor and glory for ever and ever. Amen."

- 1 Peter 1:3–5: "Praise be to the God and Father of our Lord Jesus Christ! In his great mercy he has given us new birth into a living hope through the resurrection of Jesus Christ from the dead, and into an inheritance that can never perish, spoil or fade—kept in heaven for you, who through faith are shielded by God's power until the coming of the salvation that is ready to be revealed in the last time."

I will **praise** the name of God with **song**, And shall **magnify** Him with **thanksgiving**.

- Psalm 69:30

Some characteristics of a godly woman (Proverbs 31:10-31)

A study of the godly woman of Proverbs 31 teaches women of today some valuable lessons. We may not have a household of maidservants, seek wool and flax, or bring our food from afar, but there are general principles that show us how to be the kind of wise woman that God desires us to be. Let us examine each verse.

- Proverbs 31:10: "Who can find a virtuous wife? For her worth is far above rubies."
  Do we desire to be this kind of treasure?

- Proverbs 31:11-12: "The heart of her husband safely trusts her; so he will have no lack of gain. She does him good and not evil all the days of her life." *This godly woman is honest and wise in her dealings so he trusts her. He can trust that she will not do him wrong in any way.*

- Proverbs 31:13: "She seeks wool and flax, and willingly works with her hands." *In our modern days, most of us do not do this specific type of work, but the key phrase here is "willingly works." A godly woman is a hard working woman, not lazy. This scripture also implies that she is self-directed in her work. She doesn't wait for someone to tell her what to do. She looks for work and does it.*

- Proverbs 31:14-15: "She is like the merchant ships, she brings her food from afar. She also rises while it is yet night, and provides food for her household, and a portion for her maidservants."
  In this scripture she goes out and brings food into the household. Once again, she is not lazy because she rises up early to provide food. And we learn that she is wealthy enough to have maidservants. The word "portion" is sometimes translated "task" in the original Hebrew. So it may mean that she gives her maid a portion of the food, or that she assigns them their tasks for the day. Regardless, once again we see a wise woman who is handling her responsibilities well.

- Proverbs 31:16: "She girds herself with strength and strengthens her arms." *Godly women are strong. "Strengthens her arms" implies that she is able to take care of her responsibilities. Strength implies courage. "Have I not commanded you? Be strong and courageous. Do not be terrified; do not be discouraged, for the Lord your God will be with you wherever you go" (Joshua 1:9).*

- Proverbs 31:18-19: "She perceives that her merchandise is good, and her lamp does not go out by night. She stretches out her hand to the distaff, and her hand holds the spindle."
  She has good judgment, perceiving that the merchandise is good. "Her lamp does not go out at night" implies that she has prepared well for her family's needs.

- Proverbs 31:20: "She extends her hand to the poor, yes, she reaches out her hands to the needy."
  What a godly woman. As busy as she is, she reaches out to help those in need. "As we have therefore opportunity, let us do good unto all men, especially unto them who are of the household of faith" (Galatians 6:10).

- Proverbs 31:21-22: "She is not afraid of snow for her household; for all her household is clothed with scarlet. She makes tapestry for herself; her clothing is fine linen and purple."
  Once again, she takes care of her responsibilities well.

- Proverbs 31:23: "Her husband is known in the gates, when he sits among the elders of the land."
  He can confidently take his place among community leaders knowing his household is being looked after well. He can leave for work trusting his wife to manage things in his absence.

- Proverbs 31:24: "She makes linen garments and sells them, and supplies sashes for the merchants."
  This business seems to be something that she controls as part of running her household.

- Proverbs 31:25: "Strength and honor are her clothing; she shall rejoice in time to come."
  The same way that the scriptures say we put on Christ today, she wears strength and honor. What a compliment to this godly woman.

- Proverbs 31:26: "She opens her mouth with wisdom, and on her tongue is the law of kindness."
  Not only does she act with wisdom, her speech is also wise and kind.

- Proverbs 31:27: "She watches over the ways of her household, and does not eat the bread of idleness."
  She is watchful over her household, seeing to their needs.

- Proverbs 31:28-29: "Her children rise up and call her blessed; her husband also, and he praises her: many daughters have done well, but you excel them all."
  What a joyous thought. Her husband and children appreciate her for what she does. In fact, her husband says, "You're the best!"

- Proverbs 31:30-31: "Charm is deceitful, and beauty is passing, but a woman who fears the Lord, she shall be praised. Give her of the fruit of her hands and let her own works praise her in the gates."
  Others recognize her worth and praise her. Her husband is in the gates, so it must be satisfying to him to hear the good things that others say about this godly and virtuous woman.

Godly Women: Class Preparation and Discussion

Class goals

- Increase our daily worship of God in praise and prayer
- Grow in grace and knowledge of God

Things to do

1. Find one of your "favorite verses." We will make a class list.

   _____

   _____

2. What are four lessons that we can learn from Deborah?

   _____

   _____

   _____

   _____

3. Read Proverbs 31:10-31. Read it to your family and discuss it with at least one other person. Write three characteristics that you find of this virtuous woman that you want to improve in your life. _____

   _____

   _____

4. Think of another woman from the scriptures that shows admirable qualities. Where is she found in the scriptures? _____
   What is a quality that you would like to discuss in class? _____

   _____

5. Study the readings. Be ready to discuss in class.

6. Application: We will focus this month on godly women that we admire and are examples to us of faithfulness.

Remember, study each day.

Godly Women: Daily Application

Each day this month we will reflect on godly women that are examples to us. Each day, write the name of one Christian woman that you admire and write the quality/qualities that you admire about her. Find a scripture that addresses that quality.

1. Sunday: _____

    _____

    _____

2. Monday: _____

    _____

    _____

3. Tuesday: _____

    _____

    _____

4. Wednesday: _____

    _____

    _____

5. Thursday: _____

    _____

    _____

6. Friday: _____

    _____

    _____

7. Saturday: _____

    _____

    _____

Godly Marriage

Godly Marriage: Reading

Bible Example of a Godly Marriage: The Story of Aquila and Priscilla

There are references to a couple, Acquila and Priscilla, throughout the letters of Paul. They lived in several cities, and by all accounts were faithful to the Lord.

In Rome: When we first meet them, Aquila and Priscilla were in Rome. According to Acts 18:2, the Roman emperor Claudius exiled all Jews from the city of Rome. Aquila, along with his wife Priscilla, fled to Corinth. We do not know for certain whether Priscilla was Jewish or Roman since only the husband Aquila was called a Jew. Some believe she may have been Roman since her name was a common aristocratic Roman name. Regardless, they left together. They seemed to be always together. One's name never appears in the scriptures without the other. They even worked together as tentmakers (Acts 18:3). How important it is for a couple to be together; God made marriage to provide companionship.

In Corinth: Paul arrived in Corinth and met Aquila and Priscilla there. He shared not only a faith with them but also their occupation. He began to work and live with them. Can you imagine what it would have been like to have the apostle Paul stay in your house? Imagine the wonderful conversations they must have had about the Lord Jesus Christ. I can imagine how faith building that would have been. The apostle Paul stayed a year and a half in Corinth, teaching the word of God among them (Acts 18:11). Think of it—eighteen months of teaching by the

> Nevertheless, each individual among you also is to **love his own wife** even as himself, and the wife must see to it that she **respects her husband**.
>
> - Ephesians 5:33

apostle Paul. How Aquila and Priscilla must have grown in their faith!

In Ephesus: Their later actions demonstrate how thoroughly Aquila and Priscilla had learned and applied God's word. When Paul left Corinth, he went to Ephesus, and they went with him (Acts 18:18). Paul left them there (v. 19) and he went on to Antioch (v. 22) and several other churches (v. 23). Then starting in verse 24, it says, "Meanwhile a Jew named Apollos, a native of Alexandria, came to Ephesus. He was a learned man, with a thorough knowledge of the Scriptures He had been instructed in the way of the Lord, and he spoke with great fervor and taught about Jesus accurately, though he knew only the baptism of John. He began to speak boldly in the synagogue. But when Priscilla and Aquila heard him, they took him aside and explained to him the way of God more accurately" (Acts 18:24-26). Apollos accepted the truth, and as a result of this meeting with Aquila and Priscilla, he became an effective servant of God. In the next two verses it says that Apollos went to Achaia and proved "from the Scriptures that Jesus was the Messiah." Some of us will never be powerful preachers, but we can be faithful students and private teachers of the word like Aquila and Priscilla were. Encourage young women to choose a husband who will want to serve with them as a student and teacher of God's word.

When Paul returned to Ephesus on his third missionary journey, he remained there teaching for approximately three years (Acts 19). While he was there in Ephesus, he wrote his first letter to the Corinthians saying, "The churches of Asia greet you. Aquila and Prisca greet you heartily in the Lord, with the church that is in their house" (1 Corinthians 16:19). They used their home in Ephesus for a meeting place for the church. They used their home for this purpose at other times during their work for the Lord.

> The churches of Asia greet you. **Aquila and Prisca** greet you heartily in the Lord, with the **church** that is in their **house**.
>
> - 1 Corinthians 16:19

While we have church buildings today, there is no substitute for the home as a place to help others. The possibilities for using our homes to serve the Lord are many. For example, young people benefit by adults who open their homes to them for Bible classes or recreation. People of all ages are encouraged by a visit in the homes of Christians. What a blessing it is to us when we use our homes in the service of God.

In Rome: When Paul left Ephesus, Claudius was dead, and Aquila and Priscilla returned to Rome. Paul wrote his epistle to the Romans from Greece on his third missionary journey, and he said, "Greet Prisca and Aquila, my fellow-workers in Christ Jesus, who for my life risked their own necks, to whom not only do I give thanks, but also all the churches of the Gentiles; Also greet the church that is in their house" (Romans 16:3-5). Churches in New Testament times often met in homes, and once again, the home of Aquila and Priscilla was open for that purpose.

Did you notice what Paul said that Aquila and Priscilla had done for him? "Who for my life risked their own necks, to whom not only do I give thanks..." "Risked their necks" means that they put their own lives in jeopardy to save Paul's. We do not know exactly when or how they did this. Jesus had said, "Greater love has no one than this, that someone lay down his life for his friends." This godly couple was willing to give everything in the service of the Savior, even their lives. Do you believe that they were made stronger because they had the support of each other? Think of how having a godly husband can strengthen. Read Ecclesiastes 4:9-10. Discuss with your husband how you can help strengthen each other, especially when times are hard.

In Ephesus: Aquila and Priscilla are mentioned one more time in the New Testament, in the last chapter of the last book the apostle Paul wrote. It had been about fifteen years since Paul first met

Two are better than one because they have a good return for their labor. For if either of them falls, the one will **lift up** his **companion**. But woe to the one who falls when there is **not another** to lift him up.

- Ecclesiastes 4:9-10

them at Corinth, and now he was in a Roman prison. His death at the hands of the emperor Nero was at hand, and these were his last words before he died. "Greet Prisca and Aquila, and the household of Onesiphorus" (2 Timothy 4:19). He was thinking of his dear friends who were then back in Ephesus where Timothy was working, possibly having left Rome to escape Nero's latest persecution against Christians. It was just a brief and simple greeting, using the shorter form of Priscilla's name. But Paul wanted to be remembered to them at the end of his life, demonstrating how much he loved them.

There is an interesting observation to be made from that short verse. Priscilla's name appears before Aquila's. In fact, her name is first in four out of the six biblical references to them. And that is unusual! Most references to husbands and wives in the Bible place the man first. Why the switch? We do not know for sure, but we do know that God's order of authority in marriage never changes. It has been suggested that perhaps this was because her abilities were greater than her husband's, but regardless, we know that she would have submitted to her husband's headship. Even if our abilities are stronger in some area than our husband's, we must recognize our need to submit to him, even in these areas.

May we all strive to live like this godly couple that served the Lord "two-gether."

1 Peter 3:7

1 Peter 3:7 says, "Husbands, in the same way be considerate as you live with your wives, and treat them with respect as the weaker partner and as heirs with you of the gracious gift of life, so that nothing will hinder your prayers." This verse implies strongly that we need to have godly marriages to please God and to live close to Him. The Bible spells out responsibilities both to wives and husbands. To please God, not only do I need to fulfill my responsibilities as a wife, I need to live in a way so that I make it easy for my husband to fulfill his responsibilities. Look at the commands directed to wives.

COMMANDS DIRECTED TO WIVES

* Respect your husband.
  "And the wife must see to it that she respects her husband" (Ephesians 5:33b).

  Four key ways to respect your husband:

  a. Show that you respect his judgment. Respect his knowledge, opinions, and decisions.

  b. Show that you respect his abilities. Respect him as a worker and wage earner. Respect him even when he's not perfect.

  c. Show your respect in communication. Don't nag about anything. Word your sentences in a way that does not show disappointment. Don't contradict him argumentatively.

  d. Show your respect in public. Show the world that you respect him in all things. Keep sarcasm out of your teasing. Don't disagree with him in front of others.

  Draw closer to God by *respecting your husband.*

* Be a helper to your husband.
  "And the LORD God said, It is not good that the man should be alone; I will make him a help meet for him" (Genesis 2:18). The roles in marriage are that the husband is the leader, and the wife is the helper. Helper does not mean corrector ("I'll help him with all his flaws"). It means supporter. Think of the woman in Proverbs 31 as a great helper.

  Draw closer to God by *being a helper to your husband.*

* Recognize husband's headship.
  "But I want you to realize that the head of every man is Christ, and the head of the woman is man" (1 Corinthians 11:3). This is a position of rank. The wife ranks under her husband. Headship implies that the authority is

with the man. This is not popular today, but it is still what God intended.

Draw closer to God by *recognizing your husband's headship.*

- Submit to your husband.
  "Wives, submit yourselves to your own husbands as you do to the Lord. For the husband is the head of the wife as Christ is the head of the church, his body, of which he is the Savior. Now as the church submits to Christ, so also wives should submit to their husbands in everything" (Ephesians 5:22-24). He directs, you submit. You don't get your own way if it conflicts with his. Find joy in submitting because it is how God intends.

  Draw closer to God by *submitting to your husband.*

Look at the commands directed to husbands. Live in a way to make it easier for him to fulfill his responsibilities.

COMMANDS DIRECTED TO HUSBANDS

- Husbands love your wives.
  "Husbands, love your wives, even as Christ also loved the church, and gave himself for it" (Ephesians 5:25, 28). He should love as Christ loved, self sacrificially, putting his wife's needs above his own.

  Draw closer to God by *being lovable to your husband.*

- Husbands honor your wives.
  "Likewise, ye husbands, dwell with [them] according to knowledge, giving honour unto the wife, as unto the weaker vessel, and as being heirs together of the grace of life; that your prayers be not hindered" (1 Peter 3:7). This knowledge is knowledge of God; in other words, they are to dwell with them according to God's word or as God would have them. Honor "as unto the weaker vessel" implies that he should prize and protect her like a fine crystal vase. Husbands and wives are the same in Christ, even though they have different roles in marriage. Why should the husband treat her in this way? Because they are joint heirs with Christ.

  Draw closer to God by *being respectable.*

- Husbands provide for your wives.
  "But if any provide not for his own, and especially for those of his own house, he hath denied the faith, and is worse than an infidel" (1 Timothy 5:8). It is important to live within our means, to be grateful for the work that our husband does for our family, and to support him in every way that we can as he supports us.

  Draw closer to God by *being frugal and grateful for our husband's provisions.*

In summary, let us work on our hearts so that we can become the kind of wife that we need to be:

- **one that shows her husband respect**

- **one that is his helper**

- **one that submits in all things**

- **one that is respectable and easy to honor and**

- **one that is content and grateful for her husband's provisions**

This is pleasing to God. Our prayers will not be hindered, and we can draw closer to God. As we draw closer to Him, a godly couple will draw closer to each other, and vice versa.

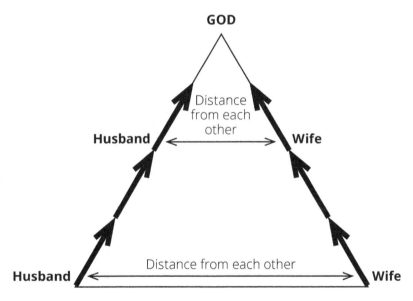

When a godly couple grows closer to God, they will draw closer to each other.

Godly Marriages: Class Preparation and Discussion

Class goals

- Increase our daily worship of God in praise and prayer
- Grow in grace and knowledge of God

Things to do

1. Find one of your "favorite verses." We will make a class list.

    _____

    _____

2. Read 1 Corinthians 15:1-2. Read it to your family and discuss it with at least one other person.

3. Study the reading on husbands' and wives' responsibilities to each other and be ready to discuss in class.

4. Read the story of Aquilla and Priscilla and answer the following.

    a. Why had Aquila and Priscilla left Rome? _____

    _____

    b. Where were they living when they first met Paul?_____

    c. How long did Paul stay there?_____

    d. Where did they go next? _____

    e. Who did they teach there? _____

    f. Name two places where the church met in their home.

    _____ and _____

    g. What had they done for Paul?_____

    _____

    h. How many times was this couple mentioned in the New Testament?

    _____

    i. How many times was Aquila mentioned without Priscilla? _____

    j. Which do the scriptures NOT say that Aquila and Priscilla did:
        1) had a preacher stay in their home; 2) taught a preacher;
        3) preached in the synagogue; 4) had the church meet in their home.

5. Application: This month we are working on our marriages.

Remember, study each day.

Godly Women: Daily Application

We can draw closer to God by focusing on making our marriages what God would have. Each day this month we will reflect on what we can do to improve our marriages. Set a goal to be a better wife according to God's word. Write it here and reflect on how you did each day. Writing it down helps you to focus more clearly on your goal. Share your goal with your husband as a first step to achieving it. Pray each day to ask God's blessing on your marriage.

1. Sunday: _____

   _____

   _____

2. Monday: _____

   _____

   _____

3. Tuesday: _____

   _____

   _____

4. Wednesday: _____

   _____

   _____

5. Thursday: _____

   _____

   _____

6. Friday: _____

   _____

   _____

7. Saturday: _____

   _____

   _____

Growing in Grace and Knowledge

Growing in Grace and Knowledge: Reading

All through this study, part of our focus each lesson has been to grow. As I write these words, I am reminded of those precious children's song lyrics, "Read your Bible and pray every day and grow, grow, grow." Could it be that simple? Well, yes, pretty much.

Except that leaves out the most important element— the heart. It can't be just a mechanical reading or praying. We have to engage our hearts. It's once again the idea of growing closer and closer to God. God is the object of our love. He is the person that we want to be near. We must long for Him.

I think of wonderful hymns that draw our hearts up to Him:

> "O to be like Thee, blessed Redeemer,
> this is my constant longing and prayer
>
> Gladly I'll forfeit all of earth's treasures,
> Jesus, Thy perfect likeness to wear.
>
> O to be like Thee! Full of compassion,
> loving, forgiving, tender and kind,
>
> Helping the helpless, cheering the fainting,
> seeking the wandering sinners to find.
>
> O to be like Thee! Lowly in spirit,
> holy and harmless, patient and brave;
>
> Meekly enduring cruel reproaches,
> willing to suffer, others to save.
>
> O to be like Thee! O to be like Thee!
> Blessed Redeemer, pure as Thou art;
>
> Come in Thy sweetness, come in Thy fullness;
> stamp Thine own image deep on my heart."

> But **grow** in the **grace** and **knowledge** of our Lord and Savior Jesus Christ.
>
> - 2 Peter 3:18

Finally, be **strong** in the **Lord** and in the **strength** of His **might**.

- Ephesians 6:10

Growth requires this longing. But it also requires patience. It is a daily, long-term effort. Consider Noah and compare him to Daniel. Daniel's challenge was immediate. Do I pray today or give in to the king's orders? Noah had to go out day after day, year after year, decade after decade, and work on the ark. At times, we will have to face dramatic challenges to our faith like Daniel, but much more like Noah, our spiritual growth comes from a day after day, year after year, decade after decade effort to build our arks, grow our faith that will save us.

Consider these encouraging words in 2 Peter 1

> Simon Peter, a bondservant and apostle of Jesus Christ, To those who have obtained like precious faith with us by the righteousness of our God and Savior Jesus Christ: Grace and peace be multiplied to you in the knowledge of God and of Jesus our Lord, as His divine power has given to us all things that pertain to life and godliness, through the knowledge of Him who called us by glory and virtue, by which have been given to us exceedingly great and precious promises, that through these you may be partakers of the divine nature, having escaped the corruption that is in the world through lust. But also for this very reason, giving all diligence, add to your faith virtue, to virtue knowledge, to knowledge self-control, to self-control perseverance, to perseverance godliness, to godliness brotherly kindness, and to brotherly kindness love. For if these things are yours and abound, you will be neither barren nor unfruitful in the knowledge of our Lord Jesus Christ. For he who lacks these things is shortsighted, even to blindness, and has forgotten that he was cleansed from his old sins. Therefore, brethren, be even more diligent to make your call and election sure, for if you do these things you will never stumble; for so an entrance will be supplied to you abundantly into the everlasting kingdom of our Lord and Savior Jesus Christ (2 Peter 1:1-11).

Growing in Grace and Knowledge: Class Preparation and Discussion

Class goals

- Increase our daily worship of God in praise and prayer
- Grow in grace and knowledge of God

Things to do

1. Find one of your "favorite verses." We will make a class list.

   _____

   _____

2. Read Ephesians 4:14-15. Read it to your family and discuss it with at least one other person.

   a. According to Ephesians 4, we are *not* to be like children in what sense?_____

   b. 1 Peter 2:2 tells us to desire what so that we can grow by it?_____

   _____

   c. What are some other things that we can do to "grow up in all things"? _____

   _____

3. Read Ephesians 6:10. Find other passages that tell us to be strong.

   _____

   _____

4. Study the readings. Be ready to discuss in class.

5. Application: Grow in grace and knowledge of God.

"But grow in the grace and knowledge of our Lord and Savior Jesus Christ. To him be the glory both now and to the day of eternity. Amen" (2 Peter 3:18, ESV).

God expects us to continually grow. We cannot be stagnant. If we are not getting stronger, we are not growing close to God. Every day this month we will read and pray focusing on growing in all things. The first week you are given scriptures to read. The rest of the month, choose a scripture each day that will help you to grow. Be sure to record them.

Remember, study each day.

Godly Women: Daily Application

It is easy to become complacent in our spiritual growth. Days and weeks can pass without us giving too much thought to our spiritual growth, but God intended for our lives to be a life-long journey where we continue to grow stronger and stronger. "For this very reason, make every effort to add to your faith goodness; and to goodness, knowledge; and to knowledge, self-control; and to self-control, perseverance; and to perseverance, godliness; and to godliness, brotherly kindness; and to brotherly kindness, love. For if you possess these qualities in increasing measure, they will keep you from being ineffective and unproductive in your knowledge of our Lord Jesus Christ" (2 Peter 1:5-8). Is there any of us who would say, "I have enough now, I don't need to grow anymore"?

1. Sunday
    Read 1 Peter 2:2. Pray for more knowledge and a desire for the word.

2. Monday
    Read 2 Peter 3:18. Pray to grow in grace and knowledge.

3. Tuesday
    Read Titus 2:11-14. Pray to live soberly, righteously, and godly.

4. Wednesday
    Read 2 Timothy 2:15. Pray to present yourself to God as a workman that needs not to be ashamed.

5. Thursday
    Read 2 Titus 2:1. Pray to be strong in the grace that is in Christ Jesus.

6. Friday
    Read Hebrews 4:16. Pray to come closer to God and find grace.

7. Saturday
    Read Hebrews 12:28. Pray to "serve God acceptably with reverence and godly fear."

Making God Our Life's Devotion

Making God Our Life's Devotion: Reading

We are nearing the end of our study. It is time to stop and reflect upon our lives.

Consider this defintion of devotion: "love, loyalty, or enthusiasm for a person, activity, or cause."

Synonyms: loyalty, faithfulness, fidelity, constancy, commitment, adherence, allegiance, dedication; fondness, love, admiration, affection, care

If God is my life's devotion, my relationship with Him is the most important thing in the world to me. Is it? Can I say that it is if I go a day or days and never give Him any of my time or thoughts to know Him? Let me put it in a positive way. If it is, I will seek to make my relationship with God stronger and stronger every day. It won't be something that I do just on Sundays and Wednesdays. It won't be something that I do just when I "go to church." I will carry Him in my heart everywhere I go.

When I think of this kind of relationship with God, I think of David. His psalms indicate a deep love and loyalty for God. But I want us to also reflect on David's devotion to God through his penitence and repentance.

David's repentance following his sin with Bathsheba is recorded in Psalms 51. The chapter begins,

> Have mercy on me, O God, according to your unfailing love; according to your great compassion blot out my transgressions. Wash away all my iniquity and cleanse me from my sin. For I know my transgressions, and my sin is always before me. Against you, you only, have I sinned and done what is evil in your sight; so you are right in your verdict and justified when you judge.

Create in me a **pure heart**, O God, and renew a **steadfast spirit** within me.

- Psalm 51:10

In Acts 2:37, when the Jews heard that they had crucified the Son of God, it says that they were pricked in their hearts. They were cut to the heart. We can see that David was cut to the heart. He begs God for forgiveness. "It is against you God, that I have sinned." The same God that he has extolled through his psalms is the same God he has sinned against.

David sinned. It is said that he broke five of the ten commandments through this act. This man who was so close to God sinned. And yet we knew that he would. "For all have sinned and fall short of the glory of God" (Romans 3:23).

> Let us hear the conclusion of the **whole matter**: Fear God, and keep his commandments: for this is the **whole duty** of man.
>
> - Ecclesiastes 12:13

Read verses 7-10 of Psalms 51: "Cleanse me with hyssop, and I will be clean; wash me, and I will be whiter than snow. Let me hear joy and gladness; let the bones you have crushed rejoice. Hide your face from my sins and blot out all my iniquity. Create in me a pure heart, O God, and renew a steadfast spirit within me."

David demonstrates his devotion in two fundamental ways.

1. He recognizes that his sin is a tragedy of immense proportions. It separates him from God. It shatters his relationship with God. It is devastating.

2) He recognizes that God's forgiveness is a gift of equal proportion. He cleanses. He wipes away the sorrow. He renews joy and gladness. He turns his face away from the sins. He blots out the wickedness. He creates a pure heart and renews us. He heals the relationship.

Surely we have all felt the pain of sin and the relief of forgiveness. Think of Peter. "And the Lord turned and looked at Peter. Then Peter remembered the word the Lord had spoken to him: 'Before the rooster crows today, you will deny Me three times.' And he went outside and wept bitterly" (Luke 22:61-62).

So we say again, if God is my life's devotion, my relationship with Him is the most important thing in the world to me. But when I damage it through sin, I should be heartbroken and begging for forgiveness.

Artist Henry Moore said, "The secret of life is to have a task, something you devote your entire life to, something you bring everything to, every minute of the day for the rest of your life. And the most important thing is, it must be something you cannot possibly do." No matter how close to God we grow, we can always strive for more. We will never get to the point where we can say, "I love God enough. I worship Him enough. I trust Him enough." Making God our life's devotion means I want to be more faithful to Him. I want to be more obedient. This is my yearning.

Making God Our Life's Devotion: Class Preparation and Discussion

Class goals

- Increase our daily worship of God in praise and prayer
- Grow in grace and knowledge of God

Things to do

1. Find one of your "favorite verses." We will make a class list.

    _____

    _____

2. Read Ecclesiastes 12:1, 13-14. Read it to your family and discuss it with at least one other person.

    a. In Ecclesiastes 12:1, what did Solomon say we should do in the days of our youth? _____

    b. What does it mean to "remember" God? _____

    _____

    c. Does this scripture just apply to youth? If one is old, does that mean one doesn't need to remember God? Why do you believe that he directed the admonition to youth?_____

    _____

    _____

    d. In Ecclesiastes 12:13-14, what did Solomon say was the "conclusion of the whole matter"? _____

    _____

3. Read Psalms 139:23-34. Read it to your family and discuss it with at least one other person.

    a. God knows our hearts already, so why would David ask God to know his heart?_____

    _____

b. How does God lead us today?_____

_____

c. Write a paragraph describing where you would like to be in 5
    years. Do you want to be a stronger Christian than you are now?
    How will you accomplish this between now and then? How you will
    spend your days in five years? Is there anything that stands out in
    your mind of what is important to you for the future? Which of the
    following four hindrances are the most challenging for you? How will
    you overcome that challenge? *1. I don't think I need to. 2. I don't think I
    have to. 3. I'm fearful and discouraged. 4. I'm lazy.*

_____

_____

_____

_____

_____

_____

_____

_____

4. Grow in grace and knowledge of God. Think of your future and how
    you will serve the Lord throughout your life. Each day over the next
    month, think of your long-term goals for your life. After you answer the
    questions, then think of what you can do to work on those goals. Write
    down what you determine. Pray and work on them.

Remember, study each day.

Making God Our Life's Devotion: Daily Application

"My long-term spiritual goals for my life are…"

Directions: Circle 1–5 with 1 being the least and 5 being the most. Each day meditate seriously on this question.

1. Sunday
   How important is it for me to love God with all my heart throughout my life?
   1   2   3   4   5

2. Monday
   How important is it for me to love God by loving others?
   1   2   3   4   5

3. Tuesday
   How important is it for me to obey all God's commandments?
   1   2   3   4   5

4. Wednesday
   How important is it for me to live a godly life?
   1   2   3   4   5

5. Thursday
   How important is it for me to be the kind of wife that God would have me be?
   1   2   3   4   5

6. Friday
   How important is it for me to be constantly growing in grace and knowledge in the Lord Jesus Christ?
   1   2   3   4   5

7. Saturday
   How important is it for me to be with God forever and ever in his home?
   1   2   3   4   5

Live With God Forever

Live With God Forever: Reading

"On Zion's Glorious Summit Stood"

On Zion's glorious summit stood
A num'rous host redeemed by blood!
They hymned their King in strains divine.
I heard the song and strove to join!

Here all who suffered sword or flame
For truth or Jesus' lovely name
Shout vict'ry now and hail the Lamb
And bow before the great I AM!

While everlasting ages roll,
Eternal love shall feast their soul
And scenes of bliss, forever new
Rise in succession to their view

Sanctus
Holy, holy, holy Lord
God of hosts, on high adored!
Who like me Thy praise should sing
O Almighty King!

This is a much loved hymn from the scene of heaven found in the revelation of Jesus recorded by John. What a joyous scene. As everlasting ages roll, all the saints that had suffered on earth shout victory, hail the Lamb, and bow before the great I AM. I want to be in that great throng before the great I AM, don't you?

"Who like me thy praise should sing." What does that mean? I sang this for years not understanding its meaning. I think it is an expression of humility. Who am I that I should sing God's praises? In other words, I am not worthy to sing God's praises. Yet even though we aren't worthy, God desires it, and we thank Him that He would allow us to sing His praises.

> **Holy, holy, holy** is the Lord God almighty, who **was**, and who **is**, and who **is to come**.
>
> - Revelation 4:8b

Understanding heaven

There are *three places called heaven*. The New King James Version uses the word "heaven" 532 times in 502 different verses to refer to three different places.

1. The **sky**, or the air that blankets the land. Genesis 7:11-12 says, "The windows of heaven were opened. And the rain was upon the earth forty days and forty nights." Where does rain originate? That is called heaven. This is clearly not the heaven which is the home of God. The word heaven is being used to describe the sky. Psalm 147:8 says that God "covers the heavens with clouds." So the sky around the earth is referred to as heaven or heavens.

2. The **planetary** heaven, the second use of the term heaven, is the location of the stars, the moon and the planets. Genesis 1 says, "Then God said, 'Let there be lights in the firmament of the heavens to divide the day from the night; and let them be for signs and seasons, and for days and years; and let them be for lights in the firmament of the heavens to give light on the earth;' and it was so. Then God made two great lights: the greater light to rule the day, and the lesser light to rule the night. He made the stars also. God set them in the firmament of the heavens to give light on the earth" (Genesis 1:14-17). Where are the sun, moon and stars? That place is also called the heavens.

3. The third place that is called heaven, the one Paul speaks of in 2 Corinthians 12, is the heaven **where God dwells** with His holy angels and the righteous of all ages. The other two heavens will pass away (2 Peter 3:10-11), but this heaven is eternal.

So when we read the word heaven in the scriptures, we need to ask: is this the sky, the universe, or the eternal dwelling place?

But the day of the Lord will come as a thief in the night; in the which the **heavens shall pass away** with a great noise...

- 2 Peter 3:10a

Anticipating heaven (why we want to go)

Read Revelation 21:1-7. Three reasons why I want to go to heaven:

1. *God's eternal dwelling*—what a glorious thought! Just imagine the joy in the hearts of the righteous when we behold God in all His glory and majesty. We gain some insight into how wonderful that will be by reading Revelation 4:8, 11; 7:9-15. In God's very presence: best company, best place, best activity.

   I really want to go there, don't you?

2. *No evil.* Just think of being freed forever from a world that is exceedingly sinful, often violent and cruel (Galatians 5:19), never seeing or hearing of anything evil.

   I really want to go there, don't you?

3. *No temptation.* Not only will we not see evil in others, we won't have to fight temptation in ourselves: no more selfishness, no more temptations, no more hurt feelings, no more jealousy. I no longer will have to fight the works of the flesh.

   I really want to go there, don't you?

We can if we remain steadfast. Read the following passages on remaining steadfast.

"Now I make known to you, brethren, the gospel which I preached to you, which also you received, in which also you stand, by which also you are saved, *if you hold fast* the word which I preached to you, unless you believed in vain" (1 Corinthians 15:-12).

"Fixing our eyes on Jesus, the pioneer and perfecter of faith. For the joy set before him he endured the cross, scorning its shame, and sat down at the right hand of the throne of God. Consider him who endured such opposition from sinners, so that you *will not grow weary and lose heart*" (Hebrews 12:2-3).

> And God shall **wipe away all tears** from their eyes; and there shall be no more **death**, neither **sorrow**, nor **crying**, neither shall there be any more **pain**: for the **former things** are passed away.
>
> - Revelation 21:4

"Blessed is the man who *remains steadfast* under trial, for when he has stood the test he will receive the crown of life, which God has promised to those who love him" (James 1:12).

"Let us *hold fast* the confession of our hope without wavering, for He who promised is faithful" (Hebrews 10:23).

"We Shall See the King Some Day"

Tho' the way we journey may be often drear,
We shall see the King some day;
On that blessed morning clouds will disappear;
We shall see the King some day.

After pain and anguish, after toil and care,
We shall see the King some day;
Thro' the endless ages joy and blessing share,
We shall see the King some day.

After foes are conquered, after battles won,
We shall see the King some day;
After strife is over, after set of sun,
We shall see the King some day.

There with all the loved ones who have gone before,
We shall see the King some day;
Sorrow past forever, on that peaceful shore,
We shall see the King some day.

Chorus
We shall see the King some day,
We will shout and sing some day;
Gathered 'round the throne,
When He shall call His own,
We shall see the King some day

We truly deprive ourselves of perhaps the greatest motivation to live right if we don't reflect on heaven often.

"Let's go home."

1. Because God is a person, I will seek an intimate relationship with Him.

2. Because God is all-powerful, He can help me with anything.

3. Because God is ever-present, He is always with me.

4. Because God knows everything, I will go to Him with all my questions and concerns.

5. Because God knows and wants my best, I will joyfully submit to His will.

6. Because God is holy, I will devote myself to Him in purity, worship and service.

7. Because God is absolute truth, I will believe what He says and live accordingly.

8. Because God is righteous, I will live by His standards.

9. Because God is just, He will treat me fairly.

10. Because God is love, He is unconditionally committed to my well being.

11. Because God is merciful, He forgives me of my sins when I sincerely confess them.

12. Because God is faithful, I will trust Him to always keep His promises.

13. Because God never changes, my future is secure and eternal.

—David Lanius

I want to live with Him, now and forever, don't you?

Live With God Forever: Class Preparation and Discussion

Class goals

- Increase our daily worship of God in praise and prayer
- Grow in grace and knowledge of God

Things to do

1. Find a passage that describes heaven. We will make a class list.

   _____

   _____

2. Read Revelation 21:1-7 every day. Read it to your family and discuss it with at least one other person.

3. Write in your own words (a paragraph) why you want to go to heaven.

   _____

   _____

   _____

   _____

   _____

   _____

4. Find your favorite song about heaven. Bring it to class. Read the words every day. What is it about the song that means the most to you?

   _____

   _____

   _____

5. Study the readings. Be ready to discuss in class.

6. Application: Striving to be with God in heaven. "But grow in the grace and knowledge of our Lord and Savior Jesus Christ. To him be the glory both now and to the day of eternity. Amen" (2 Peter 3:18, ESV).

We should always be ready to die. And we can realize that when we do, there can be something wonderful, more wonderful than we can even imagine, waiting for us. This month we will focus our prayers on wanting to go to heaven. This should cause us to center our lives on the Father so we can go and be with Him. We must prepare ourselves for the journey to heaven.

Remember, study each day.

Live With God Forever: Daily Application

"If we miss heaven, we've missed it all." Every day this month include in your daily prayers the desire to come and be with God.

1. Sunday: Dear God, I want to live with you in heaven because _____

    _____

    _____

2. Monday: Dear God, I want to live with you in heaven because _____

    _____

    _____

3. Tuesday: Dear God, I want to live with you in heaven because _____

    _____

    _____

4. Wednesday: Dear God, I want to live with you in heaven because _____

    _____

    _____

5. Thursday: Dear God, I want to live with you in heaven because _____

    _____

    _____

6. Friday: Dear God, I want to live with you in heaven because_____

    _____

    _____

7. Saturday: Dear God, I want to live with you in heaven because_____

    _____

    _____

Afterword

Class Goals

Have we:

- Increased our daily worship of God in praise and prayer?
- Grown in grace and knowledge of God?

Let us continue our spiritual growth; the class is ending, but you are on a beautiful journey from here to heaven. Think of Him more and more. Praise Him more and more. Talk to Him more and more. Let Him talk to you more and more through His word. Learn His word, more and more. Cling to Him more and more. Love Him, serve Him, adore Him.

What Is God Like?

God has revealed Himself to us in the scriptures. That is the God that *is*. Any variation from that revelation is a made-up god. We can't just decide what we think God is like apart from His revelation of Himself. If so, we are creating an idol. The scriptures say to praise God for who He is (Psalm 150:1-6), especially in song and prayer. Much of Psalms contains this kind of praise. Too often, we offer praise in just a few areas, such as God's love, and then spend the rest of our prayers asking Him for things. All attributes of God are worthy of praise. One purpose of this study is to learn more about who God is and to praise Him more and more in a way that He desires. Below is a list of attributes of God from the scriptures. (So that you can remember the attributes of God listed here, they are presented in the order of this acronym: "WISH TO FLOSS JIM EGGO.")

Wisdom: Wisdom is the ability to both devise and achieve perfect ends by the most perfect means. He is the Father who truly knows best, as Paul explains in Romans 11:33: "Oh, how great are God's riches and wisdom and knowledge! How impossible it is for us to understand His decisions and His ways!"

Infinitude: God knows no boundaries. He is without measure. Since God is infinite, everything else about Him must also be infinite.

Sovereignty: This is the attribute by which He rules His entire creation. It makes Him absolutely free to do what He knows to be best. God is in control of everything that happens.

Holiness: This is the attribute that sets God apart from all created beings. It refers to His majesty and His perfect moral purity. There is absolutely no sin or evil thought in God at all. His holiness defines all that is pure and righteous in all the creation.

Trinity (God is One in three persons): Though the word "trinity" is not used in the Bible, the truth of God revealing Himself in three persons is included. The Father, Son, and Holy Spirit are all called God, exist eternally, and are involved in doing things only God could do. Although God reveals Himself in three persons, God is One and cannot be divided.

Omniscience: God possesses perfect knowledge. Omniscience means all-knowing. God knows everything, and His knowledge is infinite. It is impossible to hide anything from God.

Faithfulness: Everything that God has promised will come to pass. His faithfulness guarantees this fact. He does not lie. What He has said in the Bible is true. Jesus even said that He is the Truth. This is extremely important for the followers of Jesus because it is on His faithfulness that our hope of eternal life rests. He will honor His promise that our sins will be forgiven and that we will live forever with Him.

Love: Love is such an important part of God's character that the apostle John wrote, "God is love." This means that God holds the well-being of others as His primary concern. For a full definition of love, read 1 Corinthians 13. To see love in action, study the life of Jesus. His sacrifice on the cross for the sins of others is the ultimate act of love. God's love is not just a love of emotion but also of action. His love gives freely to the object of its affection, those who choose to follow His son Jesus.

Omnipotence: Literally this word means all-powerful. Since God is infinite and since He possesses power, He possesses infinite power. He does allow His creatures to have some power, but this in no way diminishes His own.

Self-existence: When Moses asked who he was talking to in the burning bush, God said, "I AM THE ONE WHO ALWAYS IS." God has no beginning or end. He just exists. Nothing else in all the universe is self-caused. Only God. In fact, if anything else had created Him, that thing would be God. The Bible says, "In the beginning, God." He was already there.

Self-sufficiency: The Bible says that God has life in Himself (see John 5:26). All other life in the universe is a gift from God. He has no needs and there is no way He can improve. To God, nothing else is necessary. He does not need our help with anything, but because of His grace and love, He allows us to be a part of advancing His plan on earth and being a blessing to others.

Justice: The Bible says that God is just, but it is His character that defines what being just really is. He does not conform to some outside criteria

Immutability: This simply means that God never changes. It is why the Bible says, "Jesus Christ is the same yesterday, today, and forever."

Mercy: "Mercy is the attribute of God which disposes Him to be actively compassionate." Since God's justice is satisfied in Jesus, He is free to show mercy to all those who have chosen to follow Him. It will never end since it is a part of God's nature. Mercy is the way He desires to relate to mankind, and He does so unless the person chooses to despise or ignore God at which time His justice becomes the prominent attribute.

Eternal: In some ways, this fact about God is similar to His self-existence. God always has been and will forever be, because God dwells in eternity. Time is His creation.

Goodness: "The goodness of God is that which disposes Him to be kind, cordial, benevolent, and full of good will toward men." This attribute of God is why He bestows all the blessing He does on His followers. God's actions define what goodness is, and we can easily see it in the way Jesus related to the people around Him.

Gracious: God enjoys giving great gifts to those who love Him, even when they do not deserve it. Grace is the way we describe that inclination. Jesus Christ is the channel through which His grace moves. The Bible says, "The law was given by Moses, but grace and truth came by Jesus Christ."

Omnipresence: This term means "everywhere present." Since God is infinite, His being knows no boundaries. So, clearly He is everywhere. This truth is taught throughout the Bible as the phrase "I am with you always" is repeated 22 times in both the Old and New Testaments.

Attributes of God: The Conclusion

This is the description of the God of the Bible. All other ideas about God are, according to the Bible, false gods. They are from the imagination of mankind. By learning the attributes of God, you may praise God for who He really is and for how each of His attributes impacts your life in a positive way.